Confirm Re-Examined

Reginald H. Fuller

Michel Dujarier

Allen F. Bray III

Donald J. Parsons

Daniel B. Stevick

Leonel L. Mitchell

Iris V. Cully

John H. Westerhoff III

Kendig Brubaker Cully, *Editor*

Confirmation Re-Examined

/II

Kendig Brubaker Cully

editor

Morehouse-Barlow Co., Wilton, Connecticut

Copyright © 1982 Kendig Brubaker Cully

Morehouse-Barlow Co., Inc.
78 Danbury Road
Wilton, Connecticut 06897

ISBN 0-8192-1304-7

Library of Congress Catalog Card Number 82-81428

Printed in the United States of America

To those Right Reverend Fathers in God
ordained and consecrated in their office between 1962 and 1982
by whose laying on of hands
the Baptized have renewed their solemn promise
and vow through faith in
Jesus Christ their Lord.

Contents

Contents

Preface

In writing the Preface to *Confirmation: History, Doctrine, and Practice* in 1962 (The Seabury Press), I was able to say: "Not since the publication in England in 1926 and 1927 of the two-volume *Confirmation or the Laying on of Hands* (Society for Promoting Christian Knowledge) has the Church had a work of considerable scope dealing with the historical, doctrinal, and practical aspects of Confirmation." Thus after thirty-five years an effort was being made in that book to deal with views that had altered or developed during the intervening period.

Since 1962 considerable interest in Confirmation has been generated in all the major ecclesial traditions due to the revamping of liturgy, the reconsideration of the relation between Baptism and Confirmation with regard to the appropriateness or at least the meaning of the latter, and the revision of psychological and sociological understandings as they bear on the right age for Confirmation and its import in the life of the congregations. This interest has expressed itself in the Episcopal Church through a number of studies, especially those related to the recent revision of *The Book of Common Prayer*. It therefore seemed timely to bring discussion concerning present understandings of Confirmation into focus by assembling new essays into a volume that would center attention on this rite as it is viewed twenty years after the 1962 volume.

The editor is deeply appreciative to the distinguished scholars who agreed to contribute their learning and wisdom for this book. I am especially grateful to William H. Sadlier, Inc. for permission to reproduce the chapter from *Becoming a Catholic Christian* by Michel Dujarier, William J. Reedy, general editor, 1979, which is Chapter 2 of this volume. I wish also to welcome to this volume, as the only contributor to the 1962 book to appear again here, except for myself, the Reverend Daniel B. Stevick, who in the interim has become established as a leading authority on the Anglican usages of the initiatory rites.

Kendig Brubaker Cully

Lexington, Kentucky
Lent, 1982

Confirmation Re-Examined

Confirmation in the Episcopal Church and in the Church of England

Reginald H. Fuller

The Reformation left the Church of England with a clear and definite pattern of Christian initiation.[1] It was a process, rather than a once-for-all event:

> Baptism (normally in infancy)[2]
> Catechism
> Confirmation (normally at 14–16 years)
> First Communion[3]

This pattern reproduced that of the Reformation churches on the Continent[4] with two important differences with regard to Confirmation: (1) Its minister was the bishop[5]; (2) more than the continental rites, it focused upon the Holy Spirit and his work in the candidates, both in the bishop's prayers and in the words of administration. These two facts provided the soil for a theological development within Anglicanism, fertilized by patristic learning, quite unlike anything that happened in the Reformation churches on the continent. Beginning (as far as I am aware) with Jeremy Taylor's Prayer Book, Confirmation was increasingly equated with the episcopal laying on of hands and/or anointing that had been part of the initiatory rite in the patristic era and which became separated from it in the early medieval West.[6]

The post-Tractarians, with their devotion to the sacramental system, gave new life to this equation and to the consequent emphasis on Confirmation as a sacrament in which the Holy Spirit was conveyed. Towards the end of the nineteenth century, there re-emerged, however, a bifurcation between the "patristics"[7] and the "medievalists"[8] as we might call them. The patristics held that in Confirmation the candidates received the gift of the Spirit for the first time (with the corollary that Baptism was not complete sacramental initiation). The medievalists held that the Holy Spirit was given both in Baptism and in Confirmation. They differentiated between the two conveyances of the Spirit in various ways.[9] Neither of these two views swept the field, even in Anglo-

Catholic circles [10] and the controversy lay dormant in Anglicanism until the mid 1940s.

Meanwhile, three effects on the administration of Confirmation were observable during this interval: (1) In much Confirmation preparation candidates were taught to expect a *gift* of the Spirit (this was the teaching I received in the Church of England in 1927 and it was reinforced in the service by the singing of Pentecost hymns and the use of red as the liturgical color); (2) there was a corresponding playing down of the "ratifying and confirming" of the baptismal vows (I was taught that this was a mistaken emphasis of the Reformers and the result of their coolness to the sacraments); (3) more seriously, the spate of Prayer Book revisions that emerged in the early twentieth century[11] adopted as a scripture reading at Confirmation Acts 8:14–17 (I was taught that this was *the* scriptural warrant for the Anglican rite with its restriction to a bishop in apostolic succession and its sacramental character).

Confirmation again became a live issue in the Church of England in 1944, with the publication of the report, *Confirmation Today*.[12] This report adopted the medieval view of the "two doses." Confirmation was a second giving of the Holy Spirit, this time for "ordination to the priesthood of the laity," a new idea. A vigorous debate ensued, in pamphlets and in articles in *Theology*.[13]

Three positions eventually emerged: in addition to what we have called the patristic and the medieval there was what we might call the Reformation position. According to this, water Baptism was in itself full sacramental initiation, and Confirmation primarily a pastorally valuable rite more or less created by the Reformers (though with some medieval precedent). In this rite baptismal vows were personally reaffirmed by those baptized in infancy and the candidates, as they embarked upon the full responsibilities of church membership, received the laying on of hands from the chief pastor with prayer that they might be strengthened by the Holy Spirit in their new responsibilities. We may note further that among the patristic party there were those who wished to *retain* (or at least not alter) the current practice of separating Confirmation from Baptism by several years, while others urged that the two rites should be reintegrated into a single whole. Even here there was a division of opinion: there were those who wanted to couple this reintegration of the rite with the retention of infant Baptism, while a few advocated the radical solution abolishing infant Baptism and restricting the reintegrated rite to adults. Some of the patristics also identified the matter of Confirmation with the laying on of hands, others with anointing (although no Anglican rite provided for it).

This debate took place in the early stage of my own theological career, and I argued in *Theology*[14] that Baptism was full sacramental initiation, while catechism and public confession (rather than the bishop's laying on of hands) were integral to the whole process of initiation for those baptized in infancy. I also criticized as misleading the 1662 rubric requiring the Confirmation of those baptized as adults (why renew the baptismal vows so soon after baptism?).[15] What I did not venture to express in that letter was an insight at which I had arrived through a parish experience in 1945, when I was assistant curate at Ashbourne, Derbyshire. One of our vestrymen, a well-instructed churchman, asked me to "christen" his grandchild who had recently been baptized privately in an emergency. He was clearly, and contrary to normal English usage, using "christen" for the signing with the cross. This opened my eyes to the fact that if we were to equate patristic "Confirmation" (laying on of the bishop's hands and signing in oil) with anything in the Anglican ritual, it must be with the signing of the candidate in Baptism, rather than with the laying on of hands at the post-baptismal profession of faith. If patristic theology and practice were to be recovered, the right way was not by reintegrating Prayer Book Confirmation with Baptism but by developing our theological understanding of the signing at Baptism. Thus I arrived in 1940, almost alone as I thought, at a position which has been implemented for the first time in Anglicanism by the American Prayer Book of 1979.

The American Episcopal Church

The debate of the 1940s was largely confined to England, where the cultural problems of a *Volkskirche* were much more pressing than in America. It was in connection with Prayer Book revision that the problem of Confirmation first surfaced in theological discussion in the Protestant Episcopal Church.

In *Prayer Book Studies 1* the introductory essay rejected the view that the Holy Spirit was *not* given in Baptism but *only* in Confirmation.[15] At the same time, rather ambiguously, the committee announced its intention of avoiding any "interpretation of Baptism with water in such a way that it usurps or makes superfluous the normative and necessary place of Confirmation in the perfecting of a Christian, or would reduce the meaning of Confirmation to a mere strengthening of what has been received in Baptism." Thus the committee seemed to veer toward the "two doses" theory. Then, seemingly conscious of their lack of clarity, they fall back on the comfortable recognition that after all the Holy Spirit's operations are a great mystery! And they suggest that more light would be thrown on it when the "two rites" are ministered together.

Turning to their liturgical proposals,[16] we find the following features: In the baptismal office the prayer after the gospel includes the petition,

"Give thy Holy Spirit to this Child," is dropped. The post-baptismal signing with its traditional Anglican formula (more suggestive of the medieval notion of robor as pugnam and therefore of medieval Confirmation than of eschatological sealing) is retained. No laying on of hands or anointing with chrism is introduced. The whole effect of this service is to suggest the theory that if the Holy Spirit is operative in Baptism, it is so in an external way.

Two significant changes are proposed for the Confirmation rite. In the great prayer of the bishop immediately preceding the laying on of hands the traditional words "strengthen them, we beseech thee, with the Holy Ghost the Comforter" are replaced by "Send into their hearts, we beseech thee, O Lord, thy Holy Spirit." In the words of administration, in place of "Defend . . . with thy heavenly grace" we now have "Confirm . . . with thy heavenly grace." The effect of the changes to the two services is clearly to inculcate the doctrine of "two doses" and to make Confirmation a sacrament. Moreover, the second opening makes the renewal of baptismal vows optional in the interests of "shortening" the service.

These proposals represent the complete abandonment of the positive contributions of the Reformation, and the ultimate triumph of post-Tractarian sacramentalism. Fortunately it soon became a dead letter. When the Standing Liturgical Commission set forth its second series of proposals in 1970 a drastic shift of thinking had taken place.[17] They put forth a single rite, consisting of water Baptism followed by signing (in episcopally consecrated chrism where desired), administered with the words, "You are sealed by the Holy Spirit." This service was included with the Eucharist, and was to be followed by the communion of the newly baptized. Confirmation in the sense of mature ratification of the baptismal vows and conscious profession of the faith by those baptized in infancy was to be abolished. The introductory rationale for these revolutionary changes was brief in the extreme, and the proposals had not been preceded by any extensive theological discussion.[18]

One can only presume that the radical solution proposed by the Standing Liturgical Commission in 1967 was the work of liturgiologists, concerned to "reintegrate" the supposedly separated sacraments—or two parts of the sacrament—of initiation into a single rite according to Eastern Orthodox practice. Their interests were scholarly and antiquarian, rather than pastoral. Of course, the Standing Liturgical Commission was not without pastoral concern. They apparently thought that the need for catechesis and for a faith response would be taken care of by regular participation in the liturgy, as in Eastern Orthodoxy.

The proposed rite of 1970 may be criticized on the following grounds:
1. The formula accompanying the signing with the cross (with or without chrism) suggests that a fresh sacramental act is taking

place, rather than an underlining of one of the meanings of water Baptism. (The capital letters suggest that the sealing is happening there and then.) The Reformers, following the New Testament, would have been jealous of anything that obscured the fact that water Baptism is the *eph hapax*, full, sacramental admission to the church. Other ceremonies (such as the signing) may express various aspects of its rich meaning, but not add to it. Here is a radical departure from Anglican doctrine.

2. In providing for catechesis and public profession of faith the Reformers recovered essential elements of the patristic rite, adapted to the circumstances of infant Baptism. These elements have disappeared.

3. The Anglican Reformers, following Bucer, felt it desirable that the chief pastor should be associated with the process on initiation. This too was now allowed to go by the board where the priest presided in the absence of the bishop. The suggestion that the (optional) episcopally consecrated chrism established such an association was completely antiquarian and unrealistic. The point would surely have been lost on the average layman. Fortunately the bishops and General Convention refused to buy the whole package. Neither wanted to see Confirmation as a post-baptismal rite for those baptized in infancy abolished, for whatever reason.

General Convention at Houston in October 1970 acted as follows:

(1) The water Baptism part of the rite was adopted as a trial rite.

(2) The "sealing" was to be omitted in case of infants.

(3) The whole rite, the sealing included, was to be used for adults.

(4) In the case of those baptized in infancy, experiments were encouraged with earlier or later ages for Confirmation.

In their meeting in 1971, the House of Bishops[19] went on record as follows:

"Confirmation, as Anglicans have practiced it, is liturgically and sacramentally a significant occasion of (the) intervention of the Holy Spirit. It involves the special moment in a person's life when the individual makes a personal and public commitment to discipleship — a discipleship to which the faith of the church committed him at Baptism."

Such a rite was greatly to be cherished and not to be lost. There was loose theological thinking both in Convention and on the part of the bishops, but precipitate action jettisoning the Reformation concerns was averted.

So we come to the Draft Book of 1976 as passed by General Convention in 1979,[20] and now the official Prayer Book of the Episcopal Church. The crucial part of the rite of Baptism consists of:

1) Water baptism.
2) A prayer over the candidates. This states that by water and the Holy Spirit the baptized have received forgiveness of sin and have been raised to the new life of grace. It prays that in the time to come they may be sustained by the Holy Spirit.
3) A laying on of hands by the bishop (or priest in his absence) and a signing with the cross (with the optional use of chrism) and the words:
"N, you are sealed by the Holy Spirit in Baptism and marked as Christ's own for ever." The signing may be done immediately after the water Baptism.

Within the baptismal rite forms are provided for the bishop for the "Confirmation" of those baptized in infancy, for the reception of those baptized people from other denominations, and for the reaffirmation of Christian commitment. This material is duplicated in the section of the Prayer Book entitled "Pastoral Offices" (pp. 412–19). Two rubrics explain these provisions:

"In the course of their Christian development, those baptized at an earlier age are expected, when they are ready and have been duly prepared, to make a mature public affirmation of their faith and commitment to the responsibilities of their Baptism and to receive the laying on of hands by the bishop.

"Those baptized as adults, unless baptized by a bishop, are also expected to make a public affirmation of their faith and commitment to the responsibilities of their Baptism in the presence of a bishop and to receive the laying on of hands."

This service, like Baptism, is incorporated into the eucharistic Service of the Word, with provision for an alternative ending when Holy Communion does not follow. A renewal of baptismal vows and profession precedes the laying on of hands, both in the initiation rite and in the pastoral office.

The first rubric of the initiation service states that "Holy Baptism is full initiation by water and the Holy Spirit into Christ's body the Church." In accordance with this the laying on of hands in "Confirmation" and reaffirmation carefuly avoids any suggestion that the Holy Spirit is "given" in this rite, and prays rather for growth in the Spirit already given in Baptism.

In the new catechism of *The Book of Common Prayer* "Confirmation" is treated in the section entitled "Other Sacramental Rites." The first answer affirms that Confirmation is one of the "other sacramental rites which evolved in the Church." The second answer states that these other rites are "means of grace but not necessary for all persons in the same way that Baptism and the Eucharist are." The third answer defines "Confirmation" as follows:

> "Confirmation is the rite in which we express a mature commitment to Christ, and receive strength from the Holy Spirit through prayer and the laying on of hands by a bishop."

The fourth answer spells out the requirements for "Confirmation." Candidates must have been baptized, be sufficiently instructed in the Christian faith, be penitent, and be prepared to confess Jesus Christ as Savior and Lord.

No doubt these provisions will be interpreted in various ways and it would be wrong, given the pluralism among Episcopalians today, to force them into any one interpretive mold. Antiquarian liturgiologists will be able to find in it the "reintegration" of the previously separated rites of Baptism and Confirmation on the patristic model, though they may regret the weaker form of the words accompanying the signation (Not: "You are sealed" but "You have been sealed," suggesting that this sealing has already happened in water Baptism) and the fact that the use of chrism is optional. They may find some confusion in the fact that the later rite for mature commitment is called "Confirmation," for they will want to see Confirmation in the ceremonies following the water Baptism. Some terminological clarification is called for. Professor Daniel Stevick has given currency for the distinction between "Confirmation A" (the ceremonies following water-baptism) and "Confirmation B" (mature profession and laying on of hands for strengthening in the Holy Spirit).

It is perhaps not quite so easy to read the medieval doctrine of a sacrament of growth into the Prayer Book's provisions. Many changes in the Prayer Book, especially as compared with the trial rite of 1970, suggest that the revisers were moving away from this. Acts 8:14–17 has finally disappeared from "Confirmation B." So too has the great prayer of the bishop with its reference to the sevenfold gifts of the Spirit (something like it occurs immediately following water Baptism or the laying on of hands with or without chrism in the baptismal rite). In Confirmation B there is a careful avoidance of any petition for the "sending" of the Spirit and instead a prayer that the Spirit already given in Baptism may foster growth. Confirmation B is not a sacrament but a sacramental rite evolved in the church. However, if English churchmen in the nineteenth century managed to interpret the 1662 rite as a sacrament along medieval lines, no doubt American churchmen of a medievalist bent will manage to interpret the Confirmation B rite in the 1979 Prayer Book in the same way.[21]

The following features call for comment and critique:

1. The intention of the statement that Holy Baptism is full initiation by Water and the Holy Spirit is laudable, if thereby is meant that water Baptism is full *sacramental* initiation. This would imply that Confirmation A consists only of concomitant ceremonies that serve to underline some of the full, rich meaning of water Baptism, e.g., the eschatological sealing with the Holy Spirit unto the day of redemption and anointing to the royal priesthood of the people of God, etc.

2. However, the Reformers understood catechetical instruction and mature profession of faith to be an integral part of Christian initiation, and in this they were recovering essential parts of the patristic rite. *The Book of Common Prayer* 1979 (unlike the trial use of 1970) does make some provision for these things, but not as an integral part of Christian initiation. They are only "expected"—desirable? —optional? The Standing Liturgical Commission has promised a rite of catechumenate. One hopes that this rite will somehow be integrated into Prayer Book's pattern of initiation.

3. Several untidy aspects of the Prayer Book pattern have been cleared up. Among them was the administration since 1662 of "Confirmation" (Confirmation B) to those baptized as adults, involving as it did the unnecessary renewal of baptismal vows and profession of faith. Also there was the administration of Confirmation to those entering the Episcopal Church from Orthodox, non-Episcopal Church bodies, with the suggestion that having only received water Baptism without an episcopal laying on of hands their sacramental initiation was incomplete. This was inconsistent with the Reformers' own view that Baptism was complete sacramental initiation.

4. Bucer, as we have seen, attached some importance to the association of the baptized at some stage with the chief pastor. The rite of *The Book of Common Prayer* 1976 is open to the same criticism as the proposals of 1970 in that regard (see above). For those not baptized by a bishop it would be covered if the "expectation" of "Confirmation B" is fulfilled. But is there assurance that the expectation will be fulfilled and the person seek Confirmation? The bishop's role still needs further integration into the initiatory process, though the situation is somewhat better than it was in the proposals of 1970.

The Church of England

As we have seen, most of the theological discussion since the 1890s has taken place in the Church of England. One might therefore have expected that it would have been particularly creative in the field of liturgical revision. Such, however, has not proved to be the case. This would seem to be due largely to the very different church-political situation in England. On the one hand, the Church of England's authority to change its liturgy is circumscribed by the fact of establishment. It now has considerable liberty in liturgical experimentation but any definitive revision still has to be enacted by Parliament. Accordingly, it has not at this stage sought to replace the 1662 Book by a new Prayer Book. The 1662 Book remains the doctrinal and liturgical norm (even if it is now largely disused).

The Church of England has an *Alternative Services Book*[22] for optional use for a limited period; what will happen when that period expires is at present anyone's guess. On the other hand, within the church there is a highly conscious, theologically and liturgically articulate conservative evangelical school[23] – a spectrum of Anglicanism until recently unrepresented in the Protestant Episcopal Church. Given this, the need for compromise is much stronger in the Church of England than in the United States where evangelicalism has for so long been theologically weak. In addition, as we have already noted, there is the difference of cultural situation. Not only are the problems of secularization much more acute (as in the whole of Western Europe) than they are here, but these are compounded by the fact that the Church of England is still very much a *Volkskirche*, in which the majority of English people expect to be baptized, married and buried in their parish churches. Confirmation in the sense of adolescent or adult reaffirmation is far less the folk custom than it is in Lutheran countries of Europe. That means that the post-baptismal leakage is extremely high. Yet the post-Confirmation leakage (viz., failure to become regular communicants) is also staggering.

As in the Episcopal Church, a series of reports and draft services preceded the final form of the new rites of initiation in the Alternative Services Book. These culminated in a final report of the joint committees of Convocation in 1955,[24] which typically produced a majority and minority report. The majority favored a moderately stated synthesis of the medieval and Reformation views with a primary emphasis on Confirmation as a sacrament of growth, but with a recognition of catechesis and reaffirmation as secondary aspects of the rite. But a minority report favored the patristic view, and preferred the "reintegration" of

Baptism and "Confirmation." Notable was the so-called Ely Report of 1971[25] which came up with proposals remarkably close to those finally accepted in the American Book of Common Prayer 1979 (Baptism as full sacramental initiation, pre-adolescent communion, and Confirmation in the sense of mature affirmation of vows. Despite this, the *Alternative Services Book* rite seems very confused, at least to an outsider, and it is not clear what it really means by "Confirmation."

Six different kinds of service are provided for:

1. The Baptism and Confirmation of adults.
2. The Baptism of families and Confirmation of adults.
3. The Baptism of adults.
4. The Baptism of families.
5. The Baptism of children.
6. The Confirmation of those already baptized.

Thus the sequence of Baptism, Confirmation, and First Communion of adults is taken as the liturgical norm, even though it is far from the usual practice. The other services are break-downs from the norm. Taking the norm first, we find that water Baptism may be optionally preceded by a signing with the cross (and optionally in oil) after the renunciations (here it seems to be an antiquarian revival of the signing connected with the pre-baptismal exorcisms!). Alternately, it may be done in the usual Anglican position after water Baptism, and optionally in episcopally consecrated chrism as in *The Book of Common Prayer* 1979. The accompanying formula is: "I sign you with the cross, the sign of Christ."

Clearly, there is no attempt, as in the Episcopal Church, to equate this signing with "Confirmation A." For it is followed by a quite separate laying on of hands. This is preceded by the bishop's great prayer, recited with his hands outstretched toward the candidate. It reads: "Let your Spirit rest upon them"—followed by an enumeration in modern language of the traditional sevenfold gifts. The bishop then lays hands on the candidates with the words: "Confirm, O Lord, your servant N with your Holy Spirit." At the end of the administration, the bishop invites the people to join him in the old 1662 (American 1928) words of administration, "Defend, O Lord, . . ." It is hard for an outsider to affix a precise interpretation to this "Confirmation" and it may be that it was an attempt to cover all possible views. One thing seems clear. There is no distinction here between Confirmation A and Confirmation B, for the same rite can be detached from the normative service and administered separately to those already baptized. It is equally clear that the Confirmation rite is not a prayer for strengthening through the Holy Spirit as in earlier English rites, but a fully sacramental act, even a sacrament per se. But what kind of sacrament? Of initiation or of growth?

As I read it, the great prayer of the bishop suggests initiation, while the prayer "Defend O Lord" repeated by bishop and congregation suggests a sacrament of growth (hardly appropriate when administered in juxtaposition to water Baptism, but perfectly suitable for mature reaffirmation), while the bishop's words of administration seem susceptible of either interpretation. Of course the meaning of a rite cannot be disclosed simply by studying it. It must be experienced in the life of a worshipping community. I myself have attended only service #5 (baptism of children, though in the context of Morning Prayer). The signing was performed without chrism after the water Baptism, and the whole procedure seemed very close to that of 1662. Presumably the children baptized on that occasion, if belonging to a practicing church family, will be admitted to Holy Communion prior to adolescence (this is happening in the Church of England as here, and must be a difficulty for those who believe Confirmation is a distinct sacrament or essential to initiation as an integral part of Baptism). Those who take the Reformation position must question admission to Communion before mature reaffirmation of vows and public profession of faith (a problem which they would also feel with our 1979 Prayer Book), and the strong sacramental suggestions in the "Confirmation" part of the rite. But at least they must be content that there is provision for such affirmation and public profession. The medievalists should be happy with the stronger suggestion that Confirmation, administered as a separate rite, is a sacrament, though there is not much in the rite to suggest *augmentum ad gratiam* or *robor ad pugnam* (except perhaps—ironically—in the Reformation prayer, "Defend O Lord"!) but after all the same was true of the medieval rite.

Conclusion

When it was first organized, the Protestant Episcopal Church declared that it was "far from intending to depart from the Church of England in any essential point of doctrine."[26] How far can she be said to have preserved this intent in her latest revision? Since 1662 is the norm for the doctrine of the Church of England, it is with that book that we have to compare our rites for present purposes. As we saw, the Reformers evolved a pattern consisting of infant Baptism, catechesis, mature affirmation with laying on of hands and prayer for strengthening the power of the Holy Spirit, followed by First Communion. *The Book of Common Prayer* 1979's recognition that Baptism is full initiation (if by that is meant full sacramental initiation) does justice to the 1662 understanding of Baptism, which is that of the New Testament and the early church. As in the early church (and perhaps already in New Testament times) any other ceremonies, such as laying on of hands, consignation in chrism, etc., were strictly interpretative of water Baptism itself, underlining parts of its rich meaning. But the Book of 1662 preserved one of these ceremonies, namely the signing with the cross, and interpreted it in an ancillary sense.

Catechetical instruction was provided as an integral part of initiation in the 1662 pattern. It is also provided for in *The Book of Common Prayer* 1979, but here it is less clear that it is an integral part of Christian initiation. Clarification of this must await the publication of the rite for the catechumenate. The reaffirmation of the vows and the public profession of faith at maturity is "expected" of those baptized in infancy, but it is less clear that this is an integral part of initiation.

The provision of reception of non-Episcopalians, while involving a change from 1662–1928, with its requirements of full Confirmation, is an adaptation to newer pastoral needs. Such adaptations, as we have seen, were provided by the Reformers in their own days.

Finally, the admission of pre-adolescents to Communion (and indeed infant communion, if permitted) is on the face of it a radical change. The Reformers insisted that only those who were confirmed or desirous of being confirmed should be admitted to Communion, not—as many as have erroneously thought—because they or the 1662 Prayer Book regarded Confirmation as a sacrament integral to Christian initiation, but because they believed that mature faith was necessary before the reception of Communion. In making this change however, the mind of the present church, both in England and here, is to extend the same thinking as the Reformers already applied to infant Baptism. It is the faith of the believing congregation, rather than that of the individual candidate, that is sufficient for the valid reception of the Holy Communion as it has been for Baptism. Pre-adolescent or infant Communion, like infant Baptism, as the Reformers would no doubt have argued, should be followed later by adult profession of faith.

A Survey of the History
of the Catechumenate*

Michel Dujarier

It would be dangerous to consider the catechumenate as a reality independent of the church. There is no catechumenate without the church, for Christian initiation exists only in, by, and for the church. Likewise, there is no church without catechumenal initiation, for the church is a mother perpetually giving birth.

And, while the catechumenate necessarily involves some organization, it is not to be conceived as a means at the service of the Christian community. It is not an instrument. It is a living aspect of the Christian community, an indispensable facet of the life of the church. This is why we have to understand the content and the exigencies of the maternal function of the church.

To orient our study, let us first consider what the church is: it is a mother ceaselessly engaged in the process of giving birth and educating. Then, from this perspective, we shall consider how the church has tried to accomplish this by catechumenal education.

The Maternal Function of the Church

To begin, let us note some fundamental affirmations of the Second Vatican Council. On two occasions, the *Dogmatic Constitution of the Church* clearly speaks of the initiation of new members into the church in terms of conception, gestation and maternity:

> "Catechumens who, moved by the Holy Spirit, seek with explicit intention to be incorporated into the Church are by that very intention joined to her. With love and solicitude Mother Church already embraces them as her own." (¶14)

*This chapter is reproduced by permission of William H. Sadlier, Inc. from *Becoming a Catholic Christian: A Symposium on Christian Initiation Organized and Directed by Christiane Brusselmans*, William J. Reedy, general editor, copyright by William Sadlier, Inc., 1979.

"The Church . . . becomes a Mother by accepting God's word in faith. For by her preaching and by baptism she brings forth to a new and immortal life children who are conceived of the Holy Spirit and born of God." (¶64)

Such language cannot be dismissed as merely figurative. The maternal function of the church is neither a metaphor nor an image, it is a reality of life. And if it is proper to speak of the mission of the church with regard to Christian initiation, it is because Christian initiation springs from the very essence of the church, which is maternal.[1]

This is what the Council forcefully affirms, following the Fathers of the church,[2] in texts too numerous to cite here. The church is called "our Mother" (Lumen Gentium, ¶6); she exercises her maternity not only when she gives birth but also when she educates, concerning herself with the totality of the life situation (Gravissimum Educationis, Introduction and 3); and, moreover, her "maternal solicitude" must extend "to all men, believers or not" (Christus Dominus, ¶13).

Thus, it is within the perspective of the church as mother that we must situate all pastoral activity,[3] and particularly the catechumenal dimension. Let us try to formulate this perspective in three propositions.

(1) The church is essentially a mother. It exercises its maternal function in three dimensions of the mission entrusted to it by Christ.

When Christ, "the way, the truth, and the life" (John 14:6), promised his disciples to be "always with them," he clearly showed that the church would also have the mission to be the way, the truth, and the life (cf. Mt. 28:18–20):

- "Go and make disciples of all nations." The church is mother when it transmits the word of truth.
- "Baptize them in the name of the Father, and of the Son, and of the Holy Spirit." The church is mother when it communicates life through the sacraments.
- "Teach them to hold fast to all I have taught you." The church is mother when it leads its children along the way to the Father.

It is in these three aspects together that the church fulfills its maternal function. These aspects merge for the Word already bears life, the sacraments do not give life apart from the Word, and the way is nothing other than existence always animated by the Word and life. Each aspect, nonetheless, manifests in its own way the triple dimension of the mission of the church as mother: "She has the responsibility of announcing the way of salvation to all men, of communicating the life of Christ to those who believe, and of assisting them with ceaseless concern so that they may grow into the fullness of that same life." (Gravissimum Educationis, ¶3)

In order to be faithful to her nature and mission of mother, the church must purposely implement the totality of these three dimensions, both for individuals and for collectivities. And it must do this consecutively and concurrently:

- consecutively, because every community, as does every person, passes consecutively through the three periods of the proclamation of the Word, of entry into life, and of growth;
- concurrently, since every community and every individual, even if they have arrived at the stage of growth, always need to be converted to the Word and to enter more fully into the life of God.

It is because one or the other of these three dimensions has been forgotten that from time to time many of our churches have lapsed into passivity and formalism. And it is in rediscovering the necessity of permanently accepting these three dimensions of its maternal mission that our church will refind its youth and its dynamism.

(2) The catechumenate is one of the ways in which the church fulfills its maternal role.

The catechumenate does not exist autonomously. It springs from the life of the church and can only be understood in terms of the church. A survey of the history of the first centuries of the church will help us to understand this.

The motherhood of the church precedes the catechumenate. In fact, during the first century and a half of her existence, from 30 to 180, there was no catechumenal institution as such.[4] Nevertheless, the church was exercising its maternal function seriously and effectively. The task that faced the early church was simply that of initiating new members, the particular method was not of primary concern. Whatever may be the situation of our church communities, and independent of what we may know or think about the catechumenate, we have the duty of bringing to birth authentic Christians and of fostering their growth, and, therefore, also to reflect on the way we take up this mission.

The catechumentate is what living communities create. No decree instituted the catechumenate. Born out of the life of the community, it was lived as an imperative of the mission of the church. Gradually, forms and structures developed that were appropriate to the various circumstances the church found itself in.

From the year 180 and during all of the third century, a more definite catechumenal practice emerged for better formation of converts. Faced with the many heresies, with the growing numbers of converts, and with the risks of persecution, the church as mother reacted spontaneously and adopted converging practices in the four corners of the Mediterranean world.

In the fourth and fifth centuries, the ease of the Constantinian regime led to a certain devitalization of the years of catechumenal formation. But the Christian communities succeeded in recovering their balance by developing the Lenten and Paschal seasons to maintain, albeit under a different form, the demands of serious initiation.

So it is not a matter of advocating one or another catechumenal formula! What is necessary is that we examine the pastoral situation closely and that we endeavor to respond to it creatively.

The word "catechumenate" is incapable of expressing, by itself, all of the vitality of Christian initiation. We must be suspicious of words, however rich their content, that risk limiting our conception of the realities involved. Especially when it concerns a vital reality, a single word cannot encompass the whole.

Remember that the word "catechumenate," in the sense of an institution, did not exist in the early church. The liturgical, canonical and patristic texts on which our knowledge of the catechumenal practice is based do not speak of an organization but of persons. It was not a question of a "catechumenate," but of catechumens.

Nor were these persons themselves designated by a single term. In addition to the word "catechumen," there were synonyms more suited to the stages of their journey, for example, "auditors," "elect," and "those who ask together." Note that most of these terms express an action: "those who are listening," "those who are being enlightened," and so on. In the second century, particularly in the Judeo-Christian milieu, we find the term, "proselyte of Christ," i.e., one who is going towards Christ. And this expression was in turn reflected in such variations as "the one who is coming," "the one who is coming to the church," "the one who is coming to faith."

Finally, a number of extremely rich images expressed catechumenal pedagogy.

- The Biblical image of the "march" was developed by Origen in particular. He compared the catechumenate to the Exodus of the Hebrew people who, between the Red Sea (entrance into the catechumenate) and the River Jordan (Baptism) advanced together as a group, received the Word of God, and strove to live it.[5]
- The concrete image of "gestation" was dear to the fathers of the fourth century. They saw the catechumen as an infant who was conceived and who developed in the womb of the church until it was ready to enter the world at baptism.[6]
- The military image of "novitiate" was taken from the name for the training period young military recruits had to go through before taking their oath and going into battle.

There are also three other images that could be applied to the catechumenal journey:

- The agricultural image of "plant": The catechumen, beginning from a seed, gradually grows, until he finally bears fruit.
- The image of "apostle": The apostles, after having encountered Christ, answered his call, lived with him for three years, and then experienced his death and resurrection and the life of the Spirit.
- The image of "covenant": In the sense of the commentaries on the Canticle of Canticles, the lover searches for his beloved; it is the engagement period before the wedding.

Far from being restrained or abstract, this catechumenal vocabulary abounds in terms and images, each bringing out a new facet. Let us draw upon them to widen our horizons and revitalize what only a misunderstanding of the origins of the church could lead us to take as a fixed and rigid system.

(3) The maternal role of the church is broader than the catechumenate. In addition to being a *mater in partu* by its catechumenal action, the church must also be a *mater post partum* and a *mater semper in partu*.

In order to be a true mother, the church must continue to educate those to whom it has given birth. There is a great temptation to relax the catechumenal effort after Baptism. For adult converts, we can mistakenly believe that a long period of catechumenal preparation is sufficient. For children, we think too readily that the family or parish climate is enough to sustain their Christian life.

The church was aware of this and set out to fulfill its mission of educating *post partum*. Thus, for adults, it developed a kind of mystagogical catechesis during the paschal season. For children, it gradually evolved a catechesis to give them what they were incapable of receiving before Baptism. This effort, more or less successful at different periods of the church's history, remains a fundamental need that we shall never completely satisfy. Catechesis will continue to be an integral part of the maternal mission of the church.

Ever a young mother, the church must always be giving birth through the actions of all its members. It is, perhaps, here that some of the most nagging questions occur. Is not our pastoral activity often reduced to maintenance rather than growth? What concern have we to bring the Word to the ever-increasing number of people who are strangers to it? How attentive are we in helping along the way those whom the Lord continues to call? What care do we take to bring to birth in the life of the Spirit those who unknowingly seek it? We, collectively and individually, must ask ourselves these questions — and we must insist on them. For it is we who are the mother-church.

The church is not just a mother for its children, it is and must always continue to be a mother through its children. Each Christian is both child and mother, for it is by means of its children that the church becomes a *mater semper in partu.*

This mission of the church must be carried out simultaneously in three sectors:

- the sector of the first evangelization where the good news is announced to non-Christians;
- the sector of the catechumentate where the converts are initiated into the Christian mystery and into the evangelical life;
- the sector of the eucharistic community where the members must ceaselessly grow and expand.

The church will not be fully a mother unless it acts in all three of these sectors.

In the light of this fundamental principle, which was so strongly emphasized by the fathers of the church and affirmed by the Council, we now turn to the evolution of the catechumenate. We shall see how, despite human limitations, the Holy Spirt has never ceased to renew, under various forms, catechumenal pedagogy.

The Catechumenate: Some Historical Developments

It is not my intention here to trace in detail the history of the catechumenate. I shall only present some historical milestones that serve to shed some light on the pastoral situation that confronts us today in the last quarter of the twentieth century.

Schematically, we can distinguish four major periods in the evolution of catechumenal perspectives:

- The Beginnings: This period from the first to the fifth century encompasses both the high point and the decline of the catechumenate.[7]
- The Eclispe: For a thousand years, from the sixth to the fifteenth century, the catechumenate seems to have existed only as a relic of the past or as an ideal that was never realized.[8]
- The Modern Missionary Period, from the sixteenth to the twentieth century, saw the progressive but halting rediscovery of catechumenal pedagogy.[9]
- The Conciliar Period, beginning in the 1950s, marks the renewal of catechumenal initiation.

Without going into all the details of this rather well-known period, let us consider three principal periods that are rich in pastoral education.

(1) During the first two centuries, the preparation of converts for the sacraments of initiation was very flexible. Although there was no fixed

organization of the catechumenate in the strict sense, we can discern three essential elements:

Admission to the sacraments was contingent on two specific requirements: faith in Christ and conversion of life. The leaders of the community confirmed whether or not the candidates did in fact meet these requirements, basing their decision on the testimony of witnesses and other guarantees.

The formation of the converts was the task of the laity. Far from being a sign of carelessness, the nonexistence of a defined catechumenal structure shows that this task was assumed spontaneously by individual Christians—who took upon themselves the responsibility of announcing the Word to their relatives and friends, and of helping them to change their lives—and by the community, which frequently gathered to pray and meditate on the Word.

Sacramental initiation took place over a period of time and in celebration in which the participation of the community was essential. It is precisely the seriousness with which these three fundamental elements were taken that enabled the catechumenate to evolve into the form that we know from the Apostolic Tradition of Hippolytus.

(2) The third century was certainly the period when catechumenal instruction was carried out with the greatest degree of seriousness and intensity. This was due in large measure to the important role played by the stages and by the quality of the formation.

The preparation for Baptism was a journey marked by two thresholds, which one did not cross unthinkingly. The first threshold consisted of admission to the catechumenate. It presupposed a general though real conversion accompanied by a willingness to conform to the Christian way of life. And no one was admitted unless witnesses could be furnished. The second threshold was that of admission to Baptism and this was crossed only after close examination of the candidate's behavior. It also relied on the testimony of witnesses.

The second factor responsible for the high quality of Christian initiation at this time was the importance placed on the periods of formation that prepared the candidate.

Before being admitted to the catechumenate, the candidate had already received a basic formation covering the central aspects of the faith and had already had some experience in living the Christian life. The catechumenate stage lasted for a rather long time (three years on the average) and included community catechesis practically every day. Finally, the Baptism of the candidate was a liturgical celebration spread out over the course of a full week and experienced by the entire community in a particularly intense fashion.

Thus, throughout the third century, we find the same three fundamental elements of initiation that were present at the very beginning, only now they are reinforced in order to be lived more authentically during a longer and more communal journey.

(3) The fourth and fifth centuries saw first a tolerance of and then privileged freedom for the church. This new situation brought with it both a deterioration of the catechumenate as well as a certain renewal of baptismal preparation.

Historians generally agree that the catechumenate, properly speaking, deteriorated during this period. Why? Part of the reason was that the catechumenate began to admit people whose conversion had not been verified. To gain certain social advantages, many sought to obtain the title of "Christian," which was conferred at the ceremony of entrance into the catechumenate, but in their hearts they had not decided to follow Christ.

Thus, catechumens put off their baptism indefinitely, and ceased to come to the assembly for the required instructions. It was this lack of authenticity at the crossing of the first threshold that unleashed the decline of the catechumenate.

Well aware of what was happening, the church reacted by proposing a kind of renewal in the formation process that consisted of the creation of a catechumenate during the season of Lent.

Since for many converts the necessary conversion had been bypassed and since no formation was being provided, the bishops instituted a new catechumenate corresponding to the forty days before Easter. The examination of the candidates and the ceremony of inscribing their names that opened the season of Lent were, in fact, revivals of the entrance rite into the catechumenate. Lent thus became a time of catechumenal formation that, though brief, was intense and serious and that culminated in the crossing of the second threshold, that of admission to the sacraments, at the beginning of Holy Week. Yet, for all its seriousness and intensity, the preparation was still insufficient. So there developed the practice of continuing the formation by means of a mystagogical catechesis during Easter Week.

Nevertheless, it is difficult to remedy something that is structurally flawed. Despite its value, the Lenten catechumenate always suffered from a double weakness. First, the entrance ceremony had value only if the conversion was authentic, and second the length (about seven weeks, which was soon reduced in practice to four or even three weeks) was insufficient for serious formation since there was not enough time for real moral conversion.

Inevitably, from the fifth century onwards, the Lenten catechumenate lapsed into the formalism that foretold its own eventual demise.

Historians often explain the disappearance of the catechumenate as a result of the general adoption of the practice of infant baptism. While this did have an effect, we must also have the honesty to consider all the aspects of the situation. There were, in fact, many mission areas, especially from the sixth to the ninth century, where adult Baptism was still more common than infant Baptism. Let us look at some facts that will oblige us to perform a salutary examination of conscience.

First, we must stress that there was a kind of "catechumenate" for infants. It is interesting to note that, even for babies, the celebration of Baptism was not limited to one single liturgical ceremony. The practice of the seven scrutinies on the weekdays of Lent developed when there were many infants among the candidates. The testimony of Caesar of Arles in the sixth century is irrefutable: addressing himself to mothers bringing their babies to the scrutinies, he urged them not to miss these celebrations. This custom was undoubtedly a vestige of the tradition of baptizing infants at the same time as adults. It shows that the normative rite of Christian initiation was Baptism by stages, since the sacrament supposes faith and therefore progress in the faith.

This custom also had the great advantage of having the parents of these infants participate in the preparation for Baptism. Since the parents "answered" for their children, it was normal that they make the catechetical and liturgical journey leading to Baptism.

With the phenomenon of the increasing number and rapidity of adult Baptisms in the mission areas, there were always voices raised demanding at least a minimum of serious preparation. Unfortunately, these appeals had little effect.

Following Pope Siricius (385) and Pope Leo the Great (447), the Council of Agde (506) and Pope Gregory II (at the beginning of the eighth century) insisted that Baptisms be celebrated only on the feasts of Easter and Pentecost. By thus reducing the number of celebrations, it was hoped that serious preparation could be more easily provided. Unfortunately, there were those who pleaded that it was urgent to convert the pagans and that there were far too few priests to limit the celebration of Baptism to just two days a year.

In any case, what was most important was the provision of at least a minimal period of preparation. Among those who struggled for this reform were:

- Martin of Braga, the Apostle of Sueves, succeeded in having the Council of Braga (572) adopt a law requiring three weeks of preparation so that the catechumens would have the time to be instructed in the creed.
- Boniface, the famous apostle of Germany at the beginning of the

eighth century, instructed his catechumens for at least two months, and even longer.

* Alcuin, faced with the mass Baptisms Charlemagne was imposing by force, succeeded in launching a certain catechumenal reform. Drawing upon Augustine's *De catechizandis rudibus*, Alcuin pressed for serious catechesis. In practical terms, he demanded a preparation of between seven days and forty days.

Timid reforms, certainly, but in their context, they did signify real progress. Unfortunately, these attempts were quickly forgotten; even though they sometimes carried the weight of written church law, they had little effect in the following centuries. But the attempt to re-establish catechumenal practice centuries later drew its inspiration from Martin of Braga before turning directly to the customs of the early church.

Between the sixteenth and the twentieth centuries, an authentic movement to recover the catechumenate developed. Everywhere that the gospel was preached by the missionaries, a very strong spirit of reform attempted to restore catechumenal preparation. There was much enthusiasm, but it encountered strong resistance. To succeed, almost five centuries of constant effort were necessary. These efforts, like successive waves, washed over Latin America, then Asia, and then Africa before finally returning to old Europe. Let us briefly consider how three successive reforms culminated in the renewal of the catechumenate.

1. Sixteenth Century

(a) *Latin America*. From the 1500s onwards, the Franciscans, under pressure from the civil authorities, directed their attention primarily to mass conversion. Indians were baptized by the tens of thousands without much preparation. The Dominican and Augustinian missionaries began to counteract this situation upon their arrival in Latin America in 1526. In 1534, the Augustinians requested that Baptisms be celebrated only four times a year: at Easter, Pentecost, the Feast of St. Augustine and the Epiphany. In 1538, an episcopal conference urged pastors to return to the missionary principles of Alcuin and required a catechumenate of forty days that included fasting, catechesis, exorcisms and scrutinies. But these proposals never found their way into general practice. Provincial synods found it necessary to repeat these demands in 1585.

(b) *Asia and Africa*. The same tendency of quick and easy Baptism existed in Central Africa and in the first missions of Asia. St. Francis Xavier, at the beginning of his apostolate, baptized great numbers of people very quickly. But it was impossible to ignore the fact that many of the neophytes just as rapidly abandoned the Christian faith.

In reaction, St. Ignatius Loyola, in 1552, successfully urged the establishment in India of catechumenal houses where the converts gathered for three months of baptismal preparation. It was also at this time that the first catechisms appeared. There were those, to be sure, who opposed Ignatius in this matter, but the bishops succeeded in establishing this discipline.

2. The Seventeenth and Eighteenth Centuries

Though the victory had yet to be won, the battle had been joined. Many liturgists and missionaries tried to solidify the base of the renewal and to extend its practice.

(a) Some Notable Proponents of the Renewal.[10] Cardinal Julius Anthony Sanctorious, a close aide of Pius V and later of Gregory XIII and Clement VIII, did extensive research on ancient liturgies. After twenty-five years of study, he published in 1602 a book entitled *Restored Roman Ritual Based on the Practice of the Ancient Church*. In it, the baptismal liturgy was extended throughout the duration of the catechumenate. This ritual of 712 pages was never promulgated, though it was distributed to the members of the commission responsible for drawing up a ritual.

It was a Carmelite by the name of Thomas of Jesus who, sensitive to the needs of the apostolate, brought Sanctorius' work to wider attention. In 1613 he published a weighty tome of 926 pages entitled *On the Manner of Procuring Salvation for All Pagans* that took up the project of Sanctorius and added practical suggestions for the catechesis of catechumens and even neophytes.

(b) The efforts to establish a catechumenal pedagogy in Asia were particularly significant, but they lacked a liturgical dimension. The Congregation for the Propagation of the Faith, founded in 1622, distributed the work of Thomas of Jesus to the missionaries leaving for Asia. At that time, the *Missions Etrangeres* of Paris began to issue their "Instructions," which gave very practical advice for the realization of an authentic catechumenal initiation.

These developments formed the basis for the young Asian churches to establish a progressive journey through the stages of initiating the catechumens into the faith. Unfortunately, the liturgical renewal did not include any stages. True, certain signs were used to mark ceremonially the passage along the journey to Baptism, but they were not liturgical rites properly speaking. And finally, this progressive pedagogy gradually faded away in the nineteenth century, faithful as it was to the tradition of the church and to the needs of the pastoral situation.

3. The Nineteenth and Twentieth Centuries

(a) It was in Africa that the century-old effort for the renewal of the catechumenate was relaunched. It was a renewal whose results have now been realized throughout the universal church, thanks to the perseverance of generations of missionaries in the four corners of the world.

From the eighteenth century on, the Capuchins and the Holy Ghost missionaries strove to restore baptismal preparation. But Cardinal Lavigerie deserves the credit for re-establishing a vigorous and traditional catechumenal discipline.[11] His pedagogy rested on two key elements: (1) Preparation for Baptism must be carried out in stages, each step marking a progression in catechesis and in conversion. (2) The preparation for Baptism presupposes a certain length of time in order to assure an initiation that will lead to perseverance in the Christian life.

Practically speaking, these two principles led to the establishment of a period of postulancy (two years), followed by a period of the catechumenate (two years), and finally to a major baptismal retreat.

Unfortunately, these developments still lacked a proper liturgical dimension. The giving of medals, rosaries, or crucifixes was an attempt to signify the progress of the catechumens, but there were no liturgical stages signifying the progressive gift of divine grace. The restoration of the liturgical dimension would be the contribution of the old European continent, only lately awakened to catechumenal pedagogy.

(b) It was the example of the African catechumenate that roused the churches of Europe.[12] Its most unique characteristic is the restoration *ad experimentum* of liturgical steps accompanying the journey of the catechumen.

The church today is at a crucial turning point. The restoration of the catechumenate is something already accomplished and something yet to be done. Fundamental decisions have been taken and the plans have been made, but the real work remains.

Fundamental decisions were taken on two occasions. First, the Sacred Congregation of Rites, without waiting for the immanent opening of the Second Vatican Council, published on 16 April 1962 a decree restoring the rite of Baptism in stages.[13] The ritual was divided into distinct stages that, in keeping with the ancient tradition of the church, would sustain the catechumen throughout the course of his formation and his journey toward Baptism. This revised ritual was authorized for use where the bishops deemed it necessary.

But the text was still that of the old ritual for the Baptism of adults. The revised ordo simply divided the rite into seven parts, but did nothing to modify the rites and prayers, many of which were repetitive and not in their authentic order. Therefore, the decree of 1962, though significant insofar as it opened the door to renewal, made the need for reform of the ritual all the more obvious.

Second, the Second Vatican Council affirmed and specified this fundamental decision. The Constitution on the Sacred Liturgy promulgated the restoration of the "catechumenate of adults comprising several distinct steps" (¶64). The *Decree on the Church's Missionary Activity* presented the nature and the meaning of the different moments of the journey of Christian initiation (¶13 and ¶14). Other texts added further specifications:

- on the responsibility of the bishops to restore the catechumenate (*Decree on the Bishop's Pastoral Office in the Church*, ¶14);
- on the maternal role of the church in catechumenal action (*Dogmatic Constitution on the Church*, ¶14);
- on the role of the community in the initiation of catechumens (*Decree on the Ministry and Life of Priests*, ¶6);
- on the reform of the ritual of Christian initiation (*Constitution on the Sacred Liturgy*, ¶65 and ¶66).

The outlines of the work to be undertaken were proposed by the Commissions after consultation with the churches. In 1966, the Commission on the Liturgy drew up a provisional ritual and distributed it for experimentation to the different churches throughout the world. After an examination of the responses, the second draft was formulated and distributed in 1969 to elicit still more remarks and suggestions. The responses to this second draft formed the basis for the new Rite of Christian Initiation of Adults, which was promulgated on 6 January 1972.[14]

The appearance of this new ritual does not put an end to the research into, and the development of, the catechumenate. Quite the contrary, it is an invitation to adaptation and creativity:

(a) A guide, not a recipe. Before using the new rite, it is necessary to plumb its spirit and to understand the theology it affirms and the pedagogical orientations it proposes.[15] This is to say that it is a guide that permits different ways of application that are to be determined both by the culture of the people and by the concrete circumstances of their lives.

(b) Not a ritual to be translated but an instrument for creating a ritual. When it comes to liturgy and ritual, a valid "translation" demands adaptation, and true adaptation is, in reality, a new creation, for liturgy must spring from the hearts and the lives of those who celebrate it. This is why the introduction of the ritual leaves a great deal to the initiative of the regional episcopal conferences, as well for the style of the prayers as for the choice of the most expressive rites.

As indicated at the outset, my purpose here has been to help situate ourselves with respect to:

- the church whose maternal role both includes and transcends the catechumenate;

- the history of the church, which confirms how, throughout the ages, catechumenal action was an essential dimension of the church's life and that the church must continually be rediscovering its dynamism in new forms.

Baptism and Confirmation:
A Relationship of Process

Allen F. Bray III

The liturgy with and by which people worship is a delicate and precious resource. The form and manner we use to witness to and confess our faith is for many far more than a means to an end. It is unfortunate but true that there are many in the worshiping community who regard the *way* in which they worship as being of equal importance to the *why* and the *whom* they worship. That the style and expression should change from time to time is not surprising, even though it may be distressing to some. Liturgical revision is not a game played to relieve monotony. Rather, it is a reflection of new understandings of basic patterns and a continuing effort to relate fundamental truths to current needs and forms of expression. In the course of history some changes have been dramatic, even drastic, but more often than not they only appear to be so to the conservative person. The process and purpose of liturgical revision is, of course, a matter of greater moment for the religious communities with a strong liturgical and sacramental tradition than for those usually referred to as the "free" churches.

One of the major areas under study and, as a result of research, has experienced changes in both concept and practice is the relationship between Baptism and Confirmation. In the thrust for a greater recovery of early church custom—a common denominator which was subsequently dissipated in large measure by cultural, geographic and theological adaptations—the sacrament of Baptism appears to have been elevated at the expense of the "commonly called sacrament" of Confirmation. Beyond question is the fact that the sacrament of Baptism has always been a central and determinant point in the pilgrimage which is the developmental faith response to God's grace. Confirmation, however, is also an important stage or step in this process. There is no need or reason to minimize its significance in order to enhance that of Baptism or any other sacrament. There is a clear and definite relationship between Baptism and Confirmation which has been there from the beginning. But there are also distinctions which are peculiar to each, as Oliver C. Quick wrote some years ago:

". . . Confirmation is not a necessary sacrament in at all the same sense as Baptism; it confers further graces of the Spirit, especially for growth and stability in the Christian life, and for boldness to confess Christ and 'fight manfully under His banner,' but nothing other in kind or essential principle from what Baptism has already given."[1]

In the attempt to understand and appreciate the distinct and yet related purposes of both actions and their proper, respective places in the course of the developing Christian life, at least two realities must be recognized and dealt with. The first is the fact that historically the response to "the good news" was made by adults. We may call this an historical accident, but in no way does it establish an exclusive precedent. It was adults who first heard and responded to the preaching, who had their minds opened by the teaching, and whose hearts were moved by the healing. What they saw, what they heard and felt, was the ground, the reason, for their declarations of renunciation, of commitment, and determination. Although in the early days these may have been expressed at one and the same time, this action of response usually followed a period of exposure and instruction and was undertaken far from lightly or as a formality. They were well aware, in those first centuries of the Christian experience, of the possible unpleasant consequences they risked by even the profession, let alone the practice, of their faith. Thus, as adults, they were exposed, instructed, and received as fully participating members within a relatively short period of time, accomplishing what we have come to regard as three separate activities, namely, Baptism, Confirmation and Communion, virtually all at once. With the eventual acceptance of Christianity as a religion, however, and with the gradual lessening of the fear of an immediate end to all things, these three distinct and yet related activities became separated in time and as a consequence the closeness of the inter-relationship became diminished.

The second reality is that both Baptism and Confirmation, regardless of their place in time, separated or conjoined, represent actions which are not so much those of beginning as they are those of intent. To view either or both merely as rites of reception or initiation is to deny the full sacramental nature of the action. In this as in other areas we often tend to limit the inward and spiritual grace to the evidence of the outward and visible sign. It is true that Baptism represents a beginning, but it is also true that what is begun is far from completed at that moment. The intent, therefore, is not merely to begin but to complete, to fulfill the promises and vows that are made, and what follows may rightly be considered to be of more significance than what has already been accomplished. J.S. Whale reminds us that: "Baptism is neither an act of dedication in which the main thing is what the celebrants do; nor is it a magic rite effecting regeneration."[2] Confirmation, by the same token, is more than a rite of passage, permitting access to Communion. It was never viewed as such in the early church, but seen rather as an occasion for the assurance of the strengthening of the Spirit to accomplish the work we as Christians are given to do.

Marion J. Hatchett stresses one of the positive results of liturgical research and recovery in this connection: "Since it is Baptism rather than Confirmation which admits to communion, Confirmation can now be reestablished as a time for mature public affirmation of faith and commitment."[3] Confirmation, then, in its true and original form and concept, is not the final step in the journey to the reception of Communion, but the positive occasion for the expression of one's intent to be in the world but not of it. Again, what is accomplished in the moment of the action is of less importance than what will be accomplished in and with that life as a result of it.

Infant Baptism represents the intent on the part of the parents and representatives of the Christian community, personified in the godparents or sponsors, to proclaim a child as one of Christ's own, an integral member of that larger family of which God is the Father and all baptized persons are members, and to do all in their power to support and nurture growth in both understanding and grace. Adult Baptism, on the other hand, represents the same intent, save for the fact that a conscious decision has been made on the part of the individual for himself or herself to identify with and represent the Christian community, its love and purpose as revealed by God and received by the individual. One may be said to represent a beginning, an intent in faith, and the other a beginning, an intent in fact. That is not to suggest that there is a diminution of fact in the case of infant Baptism any more than there is a diminution of the element of faith in the case of adult Baptism.

P.T. Forsyth made what some might consider to be a fine distinction when he wrote: "In adult Baptism we are baptized *on* faith, in infant Baptism *unto* faith; but both are justified by faith only."[4] In both instances, however, the action is one of response, response taken on the one hand by the parents and godparents with the prayerful intent that the child shall come, in time, to a similar understanding, and response—in the case of the adult—to what he or she has come to be aware of as a further, a larger dimension of life and possibility. In neither case is the action initiated by man but by God, and the sacrament of Baptism thus becomes the moment in time at which a response to that prevenient grace is made.

The action of Confirmation is similar and yet different. It represents the conscious determination and the outward declaration not only to be but to do. It is, as the word implies, a sealing, an acceptance of what has been offered, challenge as well as grace, duty as well as desire, an intelligent commitment to all that is implied in such words as stewardship, evangelism and mission, not to mention ministry. Confirmation is the action which represents the intent to be on the other side of Pentecost, the point at which the transformation occurs from being a disciple to becoming an apostle. Whether this specific action takes place separately from or simultaneously with Baptism is irrelevent in the case of the person who is able to comprehend and commit himself or herself to this task. As Forsyth points out, the real distinction between Baptism and Confirmation rests in other factors:

> "Spiritual blessing come to belong to us in two stages: first, as they are made possible to us by God's grace, as they surround us and they are sealed to us; second, as they are actual, as we appropriate them, as we are sealed to them. The baptized child represents the first stage, the confirmed youth the second. The child is adopted into the home and atmosphere of these gifts, the man takes them up as duties. In infant Baptism the grace is impropriated; in believer's Baptism it is appropriated."[5]

Perhaps it is understandable that there should be some confusion about the relationship between Baptism and Confirmation as well as the true and intended significance of each action. When, in the course of time, there came a shift from adult to infant Baptism throughout much of Christendom, the imperative nature of the action gave way to a concept which was based more on a sense of the customary and the convenient. One concomitant of this shift was to make of Confirmation a more subsequent and distinct action, identified to a greater extent with puberty than with the purpose of God. Hatchett reports that many came to view the rite "as a strengthening for spiritual combat which would come with adolescence." Unfortunately, to strengthen the case for Confirmation, it also came to be viewed as a virtual precondition for admission to Communion. This, of course, was an obvious contradiction of the early practice of the church. There and then Baptism was counted as the entry point for both participation and reception. In other words, the historic place and purpose of Confirmation is not so much to provide admission to and reception of the holy mysteries as it is to provide the time and structure for an informed personal dedication of oneself and one's talents, what one is and what one intends both to be and to do with oneself. It can be said that if a baptized Christian is a mission waiting to be accomplished, a confirmed Christian is a mission ready to be accomplished.

Oliver C. Quick has noted that with this gradual shift from adult to infant Baptism there also came a greater emphasis on the symbolic rather than the instrumental action. Because of this transference there resulted a consequent lack of distinct personal investment and individual determination.[6] There developed a tendency to speak of having an action "done" rather than a process begun. In the minds of many, by the symbolic action of presenting the child for Baptism they had done their part and now the mysterious workings of the divine element would take over and complete the process. This false and erroneous view is, of course, contradictory to the content of the promises and the vows made by the sponsors both for themselves and in the name of the child. It is completely out of line with the theology and teaching of Baptism wherein the nature of the covenant relationship is set forth with a clear delineation of the privileges and responsibilities of all parties to the action.

A similar transference took place with respect to Confirmation, which came to be seen by many as more of a chronological rather than an intentional spiritual-intellectual rite of passage. Here again the popular view is that the purpose is met by the presenting of the young person to be confirmed rather than for the public confirmation of what he or she has come to understand and to believe as the will of God for the direction and the living of a life. The fallacy is that the weight of proof is now placed upon God rather than in the relationship between God and the individual, a relationship which is further strengthened for service by the added gifts of the Spirit which are sought and accepted by the individual. The importance in the moment and of the action of Confirmation is not a matter of membership status or privilege as it has so often been misconstrued, but as the point of conscious decision and the eager assumption of the opportunity for greater participation in and responsibility for the working out of the purpose of God in and through his created order.

Thus again we see that there is in terms of both the action at the time and the intention represented, in both Baptism and Confirmation, a similarity and yet a distinction. They are of course related, for they are stages in a sequential drama, yet each is important and significant in its own right. One is neither the shadow of the other nor a repetition. Forsyth, again, describes this relationship which maintains the distinction:

"Whatever is meant by an occasion so valuable as Confirmation, it is not a second Baptism, a second Sacrament, nor is it even an extension of Baptism. It gives no divine gift that Baptism did not give. But it realizes the gift, the grace that was assigned there. It does transfer most of the responsibility to the soul, and it forms a fresh step in the action of the Spirit which individualizes Salvation. It causes the man to take up the gift and its duties as his personal own."[7]

For the contemporary Christian, the focus of concern is not merely the recovery of an early and basic concept and practice, but the realization of how these two significant occasions in the Christian life are related and serve as sequential resources for the individual. Both Baptism and Confirmation are the means and occasions for response to grace, to nurture, and to opportunity. In the case of infant Baptism the response is initiated by the parents and reflects adult intention. In the case of adult Baptism and Confirmation, however, the response is made by the individual for himself or herself. It is predicated on the reception and understanding of what has been offered as well as what is required. The action which reflects the statement of commitment demonstrates for not only the church but for the world to see the solemn determination to participate fully and to represent faithfully that which has been entrusted to mortal keeping.

As Baptism, regardless of the age at which it takes place, signifies a calling out from the world and into the fullness of the life and work of the family of God, the Body of Christ, so Confirmation represents the empowering by the Spirit for the conscious decision on the part of the person to be not merely an adult but an ambassador. It is the individual commitment to undertake the corrective action which Ernest Southcott set forth as essential to restore a sense of balance and of purpose:

"It has been said that the trouble with the church, as with individual Christians, is that it is not separate enough and not involved enough not sufficiently called out from the world to wait upon the Lord and not sufficiently entered into the world to win the world for Christ."[8]

Baptism and Confirmation both are response *in* faith and *of* faith to the grace which offers separated humanity the gift of reconciliation. Each of them is a step along the way to the attainment of that unity for which we were created, and apart from which we are and shall be incomplete. The vicarious action on the part of parents and sponsors in the case of infant Baptism is no less a beginning in faith than the personal confession and expressed determination of the adult who seeks the benefit of this sacrament. In both instances, however, what follows is as essential to the completion of what has been begun as is the intention which brought it about. Confirmation, in the case of the child, affords an opportunity for personal instruction, understanding and dedication. It enables the individual to consider and confess his or her own faith and not merely that of the parents and godparents. In the case of the adult, the Confirmation experience underscores that which has already taken place, and lays further stress on both the opportunity and the obligation which is the privilege of the conscious and concerned Christian life.

Some Theological and Pastoral Implications of Confirmation

Donald J. Parsons

Criticizing someone's mother is a good way to invite a punch in the nose. At the very least it will arouse hostile feelings. For many the church is viewed as our mother, since "Jerusalem which is above is free, which is the mother of us all" (Galatians 4:26). For many other Episcopalians this concept would be a strange one, perhaps even an unwelcome one. Yet our feelings about the church are akin to those we have for our mothers. The practice of Confirmation with which we were raised is part of a tradition we love and cherish. Childhood memories include stories about a dear old bishop whose failing eyesight led to the laying-on-of-hands not only on a row of youthful heads but also on the rounded end of an elaborately carved pew. The existence of similar stories in other dioceses suggests that the legend is common stock-in-trade. Confirmation in the old way is a part of our memory, and we become resentful when liturgists and liturgical historians begin proclaiming that it was a mistaken or at least dubious practice. Our feelings are akin to those experienced when our mother's way of doing things is ridiculed. Yet feelings alone cannot justify continuing a practice if that custom can truthfully be shown to be wrong or distorting.

Scholarly research has convincingly shown that the practice of the early Church tied together Baptism and Confirmation and Eucharist as a single rite of initiation, both for adults and for infants. The Eastern Churches have never deviated from this system, and the separation we regard as traditional is in fact Western (not universal) and even in the West is a later development. Thoroughgoing observance of a delayed Confirmation in the West cannot be claimed until the eleventh or twelfth centuries. Yet "there is reason to believe that in Rome itself the primitive unity of Christian initiation was by and large substantially preserved until at least the twelfth century."[1]

We do not like having these facts thrust upon us, but the evidence is overwhelming. Despite our feelings, we must honestly ask whether

Confirmation as a sacramental act, separated by a number of years from Baptism and Communion, can be defended.

Before attempting an answer, it seems necessary to take note of a question often posed in regard to this issue. Opponents of our customary practice ask, "Is the Holy Spirit received at Baptism or at Confirmation?" The question impales defenders of the *status quo* on the horns of a dilemma and seems to bring full victory to proponents of the Eastern practice of keeping Confirmation as an integral part of the initiation rite. Quite apart from the justice or injustice of such a triumph, however, is the question of whether victory should come about in a wrong way. Asking the wrong question almost guarantees a false or at least distorted reply. This question does appear to be a mistaken approach to the problem, for several reasons.

First, it appears to treat the Holy Spirit as a thing rather than a person. A package from United Parcel Service is either received or not received. A Sacrament is (as Schillebeeckx has so helpfully reminded us)[2] essentially a personal encounter, a meeting between a human person and a divine Person. An encounter between persons is a more complex affair than receiving a package. It is affected by the capacity of response possible to the human being involved. How adequately can a human being, especially an infant, respond to the divine presence in initiation or at any other moment? There can be personal contact with an infant, and indeed personal contacts are necessary for the infant to grow into a more mature human being. Witness the evidence that babies who are held, carressed and talked to develop faster and more successfully than more neglected little ones. The infant's capacity to respond to the encounter is, however, limited. An act of the will to welcome the meeting, the language ability to spell out the meaning of the encounter, and the attendant intellectual power to grasp its significance—all of these are restricted at best. The initial encounter, however, aids human growth until the person can respond intellectually, verbally and volitionally. If Confirmation is understood in such terms as these, it is clearer that it is intimately related to Baptism, indeed that it is a part of the full initiating rite rather than something totally separate from or merely tacked on to Baptism.

Secondly, the question appears to treat the Spirit's action as capable of restriction to a particular moment, at Baptism or at Confirmation or some other instant in time. Faith is not a human achievement, as Paul reminds us, "No one can say 'Jesus is Lord!' except under the influence of the Holy Spirit" (I Corinthians 12:3). The Spirit within the adult or through the infant's parents brings the candidate to Baptism. Hearing the gospel proclamation precedes being baptized (for adults), and certainly the merciful power of the Spirit is the cause of someone's "hearing" the One who makes the proclamation effective. Likewise the ancient (and now being revived) system of the catechumenate trusts in the Holy Spirit to enlighten the candidate for receiving initiation. The ancient custom of exorcisms and "ephpheta" likewise assumes the merciful action of the Spirit.

Thirdly, the ancient practice of initiation justly cited by the critics, argues against the attempt to pinpoint the moment of the Spirit's reception. Even when Tertullian, for example, specifies that the Spirit is not given in the water but by the imposition of hands, he also insists that the anointing aids our spirit and the immersion in water has a spiritual effect.[3] Similarly the older Syrian pattern connects the gift of the Spirit with the pre-baptismal anointing while numerous Western authorities connect it with the post-baptismal anointing by the bishop or the post-baptismal signing or laying-on-of-hands by the bishop. These variations warn us against the temptation to pinpoint the moment of the Spirit's reception. This faulty form of the question should be avoided, but then we must ask what would be the right question.

The correct question, then, is whether Confirmation as a portion of the initiation rite can justly be deferred as a sacrament until years after Baptism and receiving Communion. This is not the same as asking whether it is desirable to delay in this fashion, which is another matter for consideration. At this point, the problem is whether the traditional Western (and Anglican) practice can be defended. One would expect an affirmative reply, since Western Christendom has been acting this way for a good many centuries. We really cannot indulge in the arrogance of taking it for granted that wisdom disappeared from all church members for a period of many centuries and has suddenly reappeared in this generation because we are so manifestly superior in both intelligence and spiritual depth. Aquinas was not mentally retarded.

In a sacrament we have a divine action, whose reality depends not upon human fitness but upon God's merciful promises. The benefits, however, are not received unless the human recipient is willing and able to accept the divine goodness so extended. The presence of Christ in the Eucharist, for example, is assured by his promise to be present when we obey his command to "do this for the remembrance of me." His coming, however, does not automatically benefit those who receive Communion. This fact is clear not alone because of St. Paul's stern warnings against unworthy participation in the Eucharist (I Corinthians 11:27). It is likewise shown by those occasions when the incarnate Lord was met by human beings such as Pilate or Caiaphas, individuals who can hardly be described as benefiting from the encounter. In the sacrament of Baptism, whether of infants or adults, there is involved again the issue of the reception of the mercies so graciously extended.

As already asserted, in any Christian sacrament we encounter a person; we do not receive a thing. An infant can be met by the Spirit, can be touched by the hand of God. A human being can have contact with an infant, and indeed such personal contacts are of great significance in the child's growth to maturity. The infant cannot agree or refuse to be touched, the communication is limited by the baby's inability to use language, and the intellectual awareness of the infant is inadequate. Yet the contact not only does occur, but it also contributes to the maturing of the individual. It leads to the day when the person can voluntarily welcome personal contact, can verbally achieve a vastly deeper kind of communication, and can achieve an intellectual grasp of the multifaceted meanings of such contact.

In Christian initiation there is an encounter between the divine and the human. The infant's response is necessarily limited, but his or her fuller response at a greater level of maturity will be aided by this initial contact. The multifaceted nature of the encounter, it would seem, is reflected in the richness of the primitive initiation rite, including Baptism, and anointing, and sealing, and laying-on-of-hands. Baptism in its fullness is described in terms of cleansing, adoption, regeneration, the indwelling of the Spirit, incorporation into Christ and his body the church. Does this remarkable richness of action and of meaning reveal that the early church was fuzzy in thought? Or does it not rather demonstrate that the effects of Christian initiation are so profound that they defy an overly precise definition? Tertullian, as we have seen, describes the washing as cleansing and blessing our bodies so that the imposition of hands can invite the coming of the Holy Spirit, and yet he speaks of the Spirit's resting upon the waters of Baptism.[4] The Spirit brings the candidate to initiation, acts in exorcism and enlightens during the catechumenal period, acts in Baptism and anointing and the imposition of hands and signing with the cross, and is not divorced from acting in the Eucharist which follows. When Tertullian seeks to distinguish the Spirit's action in washing and in the imposition of hands, does he not become entangled in the same perplexities and ambiguities which have so troubled those who seek to explain Confirmation as a sacrament separated by years of time after Baptism? Whether the separation is made more evident by an interval of years or is more hidden as simply a problem of theology in a single initiation, the problem remains the same. Defenders of our Western tradition must squirm uncomfortably in distinguishing precisely between the effects of Baptism and of Confirmation. What is not so evident is that advocates of the ancient unified rite of initiation are not as free from such tangles as they or we might imagine. Is it, however, a problem we have to solve, or is it a dilemma of our own creating? Do we have to "unscrew the inscrutable"?

The very same richness and perplexity confront us when we think of human response to the sacrament of initiation. The adult candidate has begun responding to the Spirit or he/she would not have come to the church, survived the scrutinies, and lasted through the catechumenate. Similarly a faith response lies behind the parents' bringing an infant to the sacrament and lies behind the presence of the worshipping congregation which administers the sacrament. It is this matching richness and mystery of human response to the Spirit which provides a defense for Confirmation as a later but not wholly separated act. The infant is encountered by the Spirit in Baptism but can respond only in an infantile fashion. That encounter aids the growth to maturity, spiritually and otherwise. A public act of confessing the Christian faith and commitment to Christian allegiance will manifest the person's grateful acceptance of that contact which the Spirit initiated at Baptism.

Is that mature response, however, what the sacrament of Confirmation means? Two points need to be made. First, the sacraments of Baptism and Confirmation have a once-for-all character about them. Confession of faith and the act of commitment can be done more than once. Indeed the story of a Christian life is a series of repeated and ever-deepened responses to God's leading. In a sense the entire tale of a Christian's life is simply a working-out of the reality of Baptism, a renewed and growing reiteration of the confession, "Jesus is Lord." Is the Confirmation confession of faith any different? Is it different as the first adult acceptance of the vows made on behalf of the child at Baptism? Now will and speech and intellect can be exercised as then they could not be. The same kind of response will be repeated frequently, one hopes, but there is a newness and a once-for-all quality about that first public and adult acceptance. Secondly, a sacrament includes a divine action as well as the human response. In Confirmation the Spirit acts to enable this decisive mature confession and commitment, empowers the action and strengthens the Christian for living out the implications of that commitment. The Spirit has touched the infant in Baptism, the contact has borne fruit to enable this fuller response, and the Spirit acts to create the commitment and empower its fulfillment in Christian living.

It is believed that this understanding of Confirmation is related to the traditional explanations of earlier times. In the ninth century Rabanus Maurus[5] taught that the episcopal chrismation and laying on of hands bring the grace of the Spirit into the baptized with all the fullness of sanctity, knowledge and power. Cyprian[6] earlier affirmed the presence and power of the Spirit in Baptism but that the Spirit was given and received through the laying on of hands. He supported this position by the example of Adam's being formed of clay by God but then having the breath of life given him. Aquinas[7] insists that the Spirit is given in the waters of Baptism but that the fullness of grace is given by Confirmation. The explanation attempted here is akin to those in that there is an implied "more" rather than a wholly different "something," which ties together Baptism and Confirmation. What is different about this present effort is found in two points. First, sacraments are more clearly stressed as a matter of relations between persons (divine and human) rather than as "things" being given. Certainly those ancient thinkers cannot be accused of thinking grace to be a "thing," but the terminology used tends to twist our understanding in that direction. Secondly, the interpersonal nature of the sacramental contact helps strengthen the writer's conviction that it is a mistake to try to distinguish too precisely that which is understood as being done in Baptism and being done in Confirmation. When human beings attempt to describe how God acts, we are bound to discover our inadequacy. In addition the relationship between persons is a complex and many-sided business which defies precise distinctions. Tertullian started it, but after all he was a lawyer. Confirmation can be defended as a sacrament of response which is intimately related in its meaning to Baptism as a part of one divine—human encounter in Christian initiation.

It is then possible to defend the practice of deferring the Confirmation part of initiation until a more mature response can be made to the Spirit's gracious drawing. Yet there still remains the question of whether the practice should be continued. Defending something is not the same as encouraging it. "Defending" sounds rather "defensive," and there are new developments in the Roman Catholic Church, particularly the restored emphasis on the catechumenate and their firm insistence that the norm for Christian initiation is Baptism-Confirmation-Eucharist for an adult candidate. Our practice cannot, of course, be determined by others, but idiosyncracy is not a synonym for catholicity. Further, an essential part of Anglicanism is the conviction that our practice and teaching should be that of Scripture and the tradition of the undivided early church. Simply because we are Anglicans we must pay the greatest heed to the overwhelming evidence scholarly research now provides as to the practice and teaching of the church in the age of the Fathers. The traditional practice of recent centuries can be defended, but we must still ask whether a better way can be found.

(1) Surely an essential step is to think of Baptism and Confirmation as two elements of the one initiation. Allowing the possible separation in time to encourage a separation in thought should be resisted. Indeed the primitive connection of the Eucharist and initiation must be held firmly in remembrance also, and this habit would enrich our understanding of the Eucharist as well as that of Baptism and Confirmation.

(2) Another obvious step is to seek as far as humanly possible to have

the full initiation rite for adult candidates. Rome seeks to encourage this by authorizing certain priests to act as deputies for the bishop in the Confirmation portion of initiation. Indeed the rite of Christian initiation of adults, approved for interim use in the United States, states that "an adult is not to be baptized unless he receives Confirmation immediately afterward, provided no serious obstacles exist."[8] Theologically we could deputize priests to confirm, with chrism blessed by the bishop, as the Orthodox do. I do not advocate such an approach. If the practice of the early church is our standard, let us stick to it and retain the action of the bishop in initiation. If dioceses are too large, then let us deal with that problem. Too large a diocese not only interferes with initiation practice but also makes it more difficult for the bishop to be a pastor for the clergy and also hinders him in other aspects of what it means to be a bishop. Delaying the Baptism of adults until the bishop comes to the parish is not impossible. Indeed it can be a helpful way of teaching the wonderful depth and mystery of Baptism-Confirmation-Eucharist, for both the candidates and the congregation as a whole. In recent years the number of adult baptisms has been increasing, and there is a special joy for a bishop to share in such an occasion of rejoicing. Reluctance to have parish priests deputized to confirm has by a few persons been described as, "The bishops want to hang on to Confirmation so they'll have something to justify their existence." Someone will find something for bishops to do anyway, so that the real question is what are the essential episcopal activities. We or they find enough other duties to obscure the essentials, and it will not help to remove one so closely tied to the real heart of the office.

Moreover, in American Anglicanism congregationalism is a barrier to full understanding of the church and of the diocese as the basic local unit of the church. One suspects that the danger is greater in this country than in some other parts of the Anglican Communion. The bishop's baptizing-confirming-offering Eucharist is not only historic but lies very near the essential apostolic core of episcopacy. Besides, keeping the bishop busy with these basic aspects of his office may keep him from undertaking other things which it would be better not to have him attempt anyway. To become a Christian is being made a member of the Body of Christ, a Body which transcends the centuries and all the limits of nationalities and races and cultures and classes. The bishop as focus and instrument of the unity of the church is an incarnate symbol of the church which exists beyond and behind this local congregation.

(3) The practice of the early and undivided church does call for infant candidates to be baptized and confirmed and communicated at one sacramental action when the bishop is present. Such behavior strikes us as strange and dubious, because of the customs prevailing when we

were raised in the church. In addition we were taught all sorts of explanations of why things were done that way, and we were taught them by priests whose knowledge and devotion we justly admired. Then too there are entirely understandable qualms about confirming or communicating children who cannot understand very much and from whom an adult commitment cannot yet be required. Infant Baptism, however, does demonstrate in a most vivid way the amazing and wholly unmerited mercy of God. The very helplessness of the baby makes it quite clear that God's love reaches out to us when we cannot do anything. In trying to grasp hold of God, we are all helpless, no matter how old we may be, no matter how intellectually advanced we may be, no matter how spiritually mature we may imagine ourselves to be. The practice of the undivided church and the logic of theological truth both argue for the full rite of initiation for candidates of any age when the bishop is present.

The major problem here, however, is not our qualms but the faith-expectations this practice makes in regard to parents and godparents and the local congregation. Infant Baptism (and so Confirmation and Eucharist) assumes that the response of the child will be encouraged and assisted by the faith of the sponsors and of the worshipping congregation, as well as by the divine action. Yet how sound a foundation do we have for these assumptions? How much help can parents or godparents really expect from the congregation in the awesome task of helping nurture the growth of that infant to spiritual maturity? Is that local congregation such that it can realistically be expected to be an effective instrument for the spiritual development of this infant it receives as a member of itself? Answers to such questions will not be easy ones. When the local congregation was a small group of believers gathered in a secret place under threat of imperial persecution, mob violence, and society's contempt, the answer could be given with some assurance. A twentieth century American parish is a somewhat different entity, and the conclusion may not be so evident.

These facts, and facts they are, do not mean we should reject the practice of ancient tradition. They do, however, make it clear that the discussion involves much more than simply a change in liturgical practice. The proposed changes are not simply a matter of altering a few rubrics and perhaps some attendant social customs. They also challenge the spiritual vitality of the local congregation and of the church at large in a most serious way. In the sacrament the mercy of God reaches out to touch the child; we can be sure of it and rejoice in it. Yet the child can never deny the fact of this encounter with him. The church is involved in that sacrament's administration, and we cannot escape that fact nor the implied duties it lays upon us. Are we sufficiently aware of the obligations we as congregations assume? Are we ready and enabled to meet them? Casual response to such disturbing questions will just not do. As we consider and debate these matters, let us not cheapen the whole business by failing to perceive how much is involved.

It is surely appropriate that those who as infants or children receive the full rite of initiation should at a later time reaffirm their baptismal vows, using the reaffirmation opportunity the 1979 Prayer Book provides. The sacramental grace has been given to inspire and direct their spiritual growth, but response to God's leading cannot be just taken for granted. There will be spiritual benefit not only for them but for the church which has been an instrument in their welcoming grace and maturing in it. A significant spiritual experience, such as a retreat or a cursillo or a church conference, has led many to say, "I wish I could be baptized all over again." The sacrament cannot be repeated, but the genuine feeling which lies behind such statements makes it clear that the opportunity for reaffirmation meets an important pastoral need. The time of such reaffirmation is an individual matter, which can be determined by the spiritual history of the particular Christian and happily releases all concerned from those never-ending discussions of the right time which plague our present Confirmation practice.

(4) For some time to come the majority of infants and children will continue to be baptized without waiting until a bishop is present for the normative rite of Baptism-Confirmation-Eucharist. The 1979 Prayer Book states, "In the course of their Christian development, those baptized at an early age are expected, when they are ready and have been duly prepared, to make a mature public affirmation of their faith and commitment to the responsibilities of their Baptism and to receive the laying on of hands by the bishop." Debate continued long and hard over the word "expected." Many, myself included, rather hoped for a stronger word, but honesty compels admission that it is very difficult to discover what that word ought to be. Reflection suggests that the word "expected" is not such a bad one after all. In Baptism the infant encounters the divine Person, and spiritual growth is rightly anticipated, particularly with the assistance of the believing community and believing parents. The mystery of human development, however, testifies that such growth cannot be demanded nor be managed. Human beings will not be programmed and will insist on going their own ways. The wonder of human maturing is found not only in intellectual and psychological and social realms; it is even more mysterious in the realm of spiritual pilgrimage.

The one danger in the word "expected" is that it might be understood as "it is expected but it does not matter very much if you do or do not do it." A seed is planted with the expectation that a pepper plant will sprout and grow and bear fruit. If no plant results, there has been loss. If the person touched by the Spirit in Baptism does not at a later date seek to confess thanksgiving for that contact and seek the Spirit's aid in the deepened response which Confirmation brings, then too there is loss. The hunger for God's nearer presence awakened by Baptism can never be fully met until we are made entirely one with him in eternity, but in the interim we will seek any and every means of having that union strengthened and enriched. The word "expected" is perhaps as good a one as could be chosen, but let us avoid any weakened understanding of it.

Yet as the "expected" spiritual maturing comes to pass, a self-chosen act of faith and commitment is fitting and right. The sacrament of Confirmation both seals and deepens this maturing response which the Spirit has been preparing over the course of the person's lifetime, particularly in the sacrament of Baptism. The bishop is the proper minister for this sacrament, just as is the case when the imposition of hands is given as part of the normative initiation rite.

Research has demonstrated that early church practice joined with Baptism a number of elements, signing with the cross, an anointing or anointings, and the laying on of the bishop's hands. Shortly a plea will be made for the importance of the anointing, but here note might be made of the Prayer Book's greater emphasis on the imposition of hands as the required action. If one must select one element, for the sake of simplicity or for other reasons, then this would appear to be the right one. The biblical instances of the laying-on-of-hands by Jesus and by the apostles are too numerous to be recounted. Further, it is true that signing with the cross or anointing do require the hands of the officiant. You cannot anoint without touching, nor sign a forehead either. By virtue of his office the bishop links the local church to the church in all the centuries reaching back to the earliest believers, and he links the local church to every other portion of the Body of Christ throughout the world, in Africa and Asia, behind iron curtains and bamboo curtains and jungle screens, across all the lines which tragically seek to separate races or classes or social groups. It is right that the bishop's hands are laid on one's head as the Spirit enables the confession, "I have been made a child of God by Baptism, I'm glad of that, and I want to live out that wonderful truth in a mature and committed service."

The vexatious question of the proper age for Confirmation can be put in a better context as the church sees more clearly the implications of the initiation practice of the early church. Permitting the receiving of Communion also eases the pressure. It seems, therefore, that seeking Confirmation can be determined and should be determined on an individual basis. There is a unique aspect to the spiritual pilgrimage of each Christian; the path of growth and the pace of growth will have many variations. The newer, and yet more ancient, understanding of

Confirmation can give a flexibility greater than what we felt we possessed years ago. Let us welcome this freedom and use it for more delicate and individual pastoral care and spiritual direction.

(5) The use of chrism blessed by the bishop is authorized in the 1979 Prayer Book. This fact is a cause for thanksgiving, but a plea must be made for the widest possible use of this opportunity. An impressive aspect of the initiation rite of the early and undivided church is its marvelous richness. Surely that richness is fitting, when we think of the wondrous nature of what is happening. All that Christ Jesus has done for us is here applied to a mere human creature, whether a helpless babe or a smiling child or an adult who acknowledges that he or she is not a self-sufficient being but a mere creature who needs the mercy of God. Here one is made a child of God, a son or daughter of the eternal Father, a member of Christ, and an inheritor of the kingdom of God. Here is forgiveness of sins, the washing away of guilt, the adoption of sonship, incorporation into Christ, and the indwelling of the Holy Spirit. How right, then, that every means is sought to manifest the wonder of what God is doing. So we have washing, anointing, signing with the cross, the imposition of hands, and many other actions too. Why impoverish that? Why seek to ascertain the irreducible minimum which we will grudgingly perform in as swift and bare a way as we can?

The use of oil is a little strange in our American culture. Of course we have ointments and unguents and moisturizing creams and deodorants and after-shave lotions and sun-tan preparations, the annual cost of which could feed thousands of the starving or educate hundreds of illiterates, but perhaps that is another matter. If anointing with oil is rather strange, it is even more strange that God should desire me to be his child and a member of his household. The biblical imagery of anointing with oil is so rich, recalling the Good Samaritan's care for the mugged traveller, the anointing of Jesus' feet at Bethany, and so many other treasured incidents. There is also the descent of the Spirit upon Jesus as he came up out of the waters of Jordan. Above all, there is the truth that Christ is the anointed one and that a Christian is by union with him an anointed priest and king. The very name of Christian, the name we treasure, means anointed.

It seems likely that those who feel uneasy about the use of chrism or are opposed to it, are affected not only by its strangeness but also by its obviously material quality. Of course water and hands are also material, but familiarity may in part conceal that quality. The very materiality of the oil, however, has something to contribute. The sacraments use outward and visible signs to symbolize and to assure the transmittal of inward and spiritual grace. The seeming offensiveness of material instruments can and does remind us that we are not angels but creatures of flesh and blood into whom God has breathed natural life and spiritual life. We are as grubby as clods of earth, a basket of potatoes, or a herd of cows. In addition we have disobeyed our Father in ways that other creatures cannot achieve. Yet to us God deigns to come, and to come with mercy and blessing. In the parched and dusty world of the Bible, oil means solace and gentleness and the easing of hurts. We too are scratched and parched and rubbed raw, and the healing goodness of the Lord flows over us like oil. In addition, we are anointed "kings and priests unto our God." As an earthly sovereign is anointed at a coronation, we are made kings or queens as we are made members of Christ the eternal king.

Attempts have been made to claim that anointing was a later addition to the baptismal washing by the influence of those many New Testament references to Christians as anointed ones. Aidan Kavanagh[9] has, however, given an impressive and powerful rebuttal which deserves attention. In the world of the earliest believers bathing was more than just washing. Among the remains of the Graeco-Roman world, the most impressive monuments are not just stadia and triumphal arches; the Roman baths are often more remarkable. To wash without using oil would for them be an experience of bareness and deprivation rather than a fitting expression of graciousness and kindness. As Kavanagh remarks, "The bath was a personal and, often, a social ritual the significance of which the modern world is perhaps only beginning to recover."[10] The whole presentation made by this eminent scholar is deserving of close attention. The restoration of chrism to our Baptismal and Confirmation rites is more than adherence to early church practice; it is a splendid opportunity which should not be missed.

(6) The 1979 Prayer Book provides appropriate prayers for Confirmation, reception and reaffirmation. It does not specify, however, what should be done with those who come into the Episcopal Church from other Christian groups. Since Baptism should not be repeated, we should not re-baptize or baptize anyone who has received Christian Baptism elsewhere. Similarly we receive, but do not re-confirm, anyone who has received the sacrament of Confirmation at the hands of a bishop in a church which retains the historic episcopate. What then should be expected of those who come into the Episcopal Church from any of the various communions in the Protestant tradition? There are those who would advocate simply receiving such persons if they have been "confirmed" in their former church allegiance. Certainly the spirit of charity and respect which stimulates this opinion is admirable. Charity, however, may be mistaken if there are other factors to be considered, or it may even be a condescending affair.

The most prevalent view of Confirmation in Protestant thought does not consider Confirmation to be a sacrament. In such a case we are not dealing with the same thing, even though the same name is used. Where that is the case, the Confirmation of such persons is the right approach. Further, a sacrament is not simply a matter involving God and the individual. The church is an instrumentality used by God in the administration of every sacrament. There is an ecclesial element in every sacrament. Someone coming into the Episcopal Church from a Protestant communion is by so doing accepting as true and important the Anglican teaching about the historic episcopate. Repeatedly the Anglican Communion as a whole and the Episcopal Church in particular have declared their conviction that the historic episcopate is one of those elements which must be included in any adequate picture of the reunited church which the ecumenical effort is seeking. Since the person involved is seeking to live out his or her Christian calling in this church, Confirmation by a bishop in the historic succession does appear to be right and necessary.

Yet again it deserves notice that Christian initiation when the Church was undivided did include washing, the imposition of the bishop's hands, and Communion. The second element is missing for those baptized in the Protestant churches just as it is for Episcopalians whose initiation consisted of Baptism alone. Charity is noble, but so is honesty. The Confirmation of persons coming into this church from Christian churches which do not practice the sacrament of Confirmation does not depreciate the reality of their Baptism nor of their spiritual growth. Indeed one would hope that their seeking to become Episcopalians is motivated by their spiritual pilgrimage, is a testimonial to spiritual growth and to longing for more, rather than the result of lesser motives. Similarly, one would hope that an Episcopalian who goes elsewhere is doing so in search of spiritual advance, which implies that at least a longing for God has been implanted by his/her life in this communion.

Clarifying the rationale for our desiring Confirmation for such persons is even more necessary now that we have officially adopted the mutual affirmation of members, proposed to its member churches by the Consultation of Church Union. This affirmation confesses "that all who are baptized into Christ are members of his universal Church and belong to and share in his ministry through the people of the one God, Father, Son and Holy Spirit."[11] Those baptized in other communions with water in the name of the Blessed Trinity are indeed members of Christ and of his church. They are not to be re-baptized nor to be regarded as less-than-Christian.

Our official acceptance of this affirmation might on first glance seem to exclude confirming of persons coming to us from other churches, but such is not the case. Along with the affirmation came an "Inquiry about the Implications of This Affirmation," a much longer document which has not yet received official response from the church as a whole. The Implications document does raise questions about Confirmation, does not answer those questions, and urges the member churches to begin serious discussion of them. Unilateral conclusions by individual bishops or priests before action by the church would seem inappropriate at the least. The Implications document asks questions about such "impediments" as "insistence on denominational Confirmation."[12] There are, it is believed, forms of denominational confirmation, but our teaching would view the sacrament of Confirmation as a part of the catholic tradition and not as a denominational affair. Furthermore, the word "membership" is a perplexing one which can be, and indeed is, used with several levels of meaning. The affirmation itself recognizes this confusion. The inquiry further asks whether this mutual recognition of membership does not "imply a new appreciation of the importance of confirming, nurturing, and instructing each member."[13] The Affirmation does rightly leave room for such concerns as long as they do not undercut the reality of our recognition of the membership in Christ conferred by God's action in Baptism. The sacrament of Confirmation does not challenge that essential truth.

Charity does not deprive someone of the grace available in a sacrament. At the same time honesty tries to face squarely the truth that there are differences in the theology of the sacraments and the theology of holy orders existing between the churches in divided Christendom. Our divisions are a scandal, and we must long for the day when again united we find together a clearer understanding of things which now divide us. Painful honesty will, it is believed, in the long run prove a stimulus to that ecumenical unity we desire and which our Lord intends even more strongly than we do. The one thing to avoid is any presentation of a sacrament which seems to suggest we are superior to someone else. An essential truth of a sacrament is that we need from God that which we cannot ourselves create or earn or use as a claim on his mercy.

(7)   In an undivided church the membership has a greater likelihood of rightly perceiving the mind of Christ. Within our present-day divisions there is much greater opportunity for any particular group of Christians to overemphasize one facet of the truth and to lose sight of another facet which needs to be held in tension with the first. So there is good sense in the Anglican effort to conform our teaching and practice to that of the early and undivided church. Of course the rightness of that endeavor does not guarantee that our understanding of the early church is correct. The attempt, however, is still right. We must therefore pay particular heed when research reveals some discrepancy between our customary practice and that of the church of the Fathers. We cannot

rightly avoid the need to re-examine our theology and practice of Confirmation.

How we may best respond to this challenge has not yet achieved a consensus within our ranks. In time the church may decide to press for the practice of the Orthodox Churches, for the restoration of a significant catechumenate with the delaying of Baptism-Confirmation to a later age, or some other option. Until that church-wide consensus is developed, however, there is a special need for self-restraint and for pastoral sensitivity. At issue is much more than merely changing a few rubrics. Changes in the liturgical and sacramental life of the church should be neither hasty nor an elitist imposing on others. Idiosyncratic actions by a bishop or priest will not assist in reaching a consensus, and we must remember that the wisdom of the whole church far transcends the insight of any individual. Neither can someone's liturgical or theological knowledge, no matter how just may be the claim of it, justify treating any of the faithful with harshness or contempt. Our real concerns are the wonder of what God does in adopting us in Christ Jesus and the mystery of spiritual growth in his children. Being correct or up-to-date or theologically sophisticated is mere dung if it leads to treating people in ways which do not encourage their life in Christ and his body the church. The Western practice of Confirmation has centuries of history behind it, and the theological and pastoral reasons for it must have had some foundation in the realities of spiritual growth. Surely our recent experience in this country of the traumatic effects of changing the Liturgy should have taught us something. When Baptism and Confirmation are being re-examined, the need for restraint and patience and sensitivity and humility is very clear indeed.

The Liturgics of Confirmation

Daniel B. Stevick

For many years discussions of Confirmation have been punctuated by words such as "problem" or "crisis." Effective liturgy requires three things: (1) clear, strong, coherent words and actions, which (2) enact the Christian gospel, and which (3) provide an interpretation of our own experience. When ritual no longer speaks clearly of the order of reality understood in the church and fails to interpret the actualities of life, it sets up what might be called "liturgical dissonance." Under such conditions, the effort to keep a rite going and to bring credibility and authority to it can be frustrating. Very widely in Anglicanism (and indeed, in those churches of the West whose initiatory practice has used the "staged-out" pattern of infant Baptism plus adolescent Confirmation), pastors, teachers, parents and scholars have complained that their explanations of Confirmation and their efforts to make it effective have a run upon stubborn contradictions.

The recent revisions of liturgy in the Episcopal Church and elsewhere have provided an occasion to examine critically the actions and rationale of Christian initiatory rites and to introduce modifications. Although the changes in the 1979 Prayer Book are modest, they are arguably the most significant structural or functional changes in any Prayer Book rite since 1552. These changes and their intention are not widely understood. The rites themselves contain some evidence of the compromise inevitable when liturgical revision is brought about by a participatory process. Whether the new rites will in some measure relieve the frustration of parishes and families and whether or not the directions taken in the revisions of this mid-century will be sustained in liturgical changes yet to come, only the future can tell. Sympathetic attention needs to be given to the rites now in hand and to the intentions that lie behind them.

The approach here will be historical. Liturgical rites carry their past with them, and the initiatory events of Baptism, Confirmation and First Communion have been little changed since the sixteenth century. Significant revision puts us in touch with the originating moments of the tradition in which we stand. History has given us both the problems we acutely feel and the resource for going beyond them.

The Formation of the Prayer Book Tradition

The first English Prayer Book was issued in 1549 containing a brief service of "Confirmation."[1] No liturgical setting is specified. Children are brought to the bishop by a godparent who serves as witness. After versicles and responses, the bishop prays for the Holy Spirit, using a great prayer which lies deep in the Western liturgical tradition. He continues with a shorter prayer: "Sign them, O Lord, and mark them to be thine for ever, by the virtue of the holy cross and passion. Confirm and strengthen them with the inward unction of the Holy Ghost, mercifully unto everlasting life. Amen." Then the bishop signs each one on the forehead, lays his hand on the head of each one, and says: "N., I sign thee with the sign of the cross, and lay my hand upon thee. In the name of the Father and of the Son and of the Holy Ghost. Amen." After this has been done to all the children, the bishop pronounces the peace of the Lord, offers a prayer for God's continued support, and gives the children a blessing.

This rite follows that of the medieval service books. In the central action, however, the bishop's signing of the forehead and laying on of hands replaces the anointing with chrism. Just why the instrument of the rite was changed from anointing to the imposition of hands is not clear. Certainly many persons of Reformed convictions in England and on the Continent had attacked Confirmation—often with heavy sarcasm—as a sacrament of human contrivance which introduced a material thing (the chrism) which had no warrant in holy Scripture. Such polemics had brought the act of anointing into question. The New Testament and other early Christian sources speak of blessing, bonding and commissioning as enacted by the imposition of hands. From the time of this Prayer Book, Anglicanism has regarded the laying on of hands as a sufficient and appropriate "form" for Confirmation.

The emphasis in this 1549 rite falls on divine action through the bishop. The bishop's prayer asks God to "sign them," to "mark them to be thine," and to "confirm and strengthen them." The bishop's indicative formula says "I sign thee . . . and lay my hand on thee."

The pastoral function of this rite is stated in extensive opening and closing rubrics. It is intended for those who are "of perfect age" and are hence subject to the temptations and perils of adulthood. It provides an occasion for children who had been baptized in infancy to ratify "with their own mouth and with their own consent, openly before the church" the faith that had been pledged by their godparents. Thus Confirmation was to be administered to those who could say the creed, the Lord's

Prayer and the Ten Commandments in English and answer questions from a short catechism which was printed with the Confirmation rite itself. No one was to be admitted to Communion without having been confirmed.

This brief description of the 1549 Confirmation rite may suggest the presence in it of internal tension between the function the rite was meant to serve and the liturgical material it utilized. Confirmation was intended as an occasion for ratifying the promises of Baptism, but in the actual service no vows were expressly ratified. This catechetical, developmental moment was ritualized through prayers and actions which had an origin in a quite different purpose. The medieval Confirmation derived from the prayer for the gifts of the Spirit and the imposition of the hand as a gesture of signing or marking—actions which came in the early church's baptismal liturgy immediately after the Baptism itself. In early Christian practice this post-baptismal seal was administered, in the East and in those parts of the West outside the immediate influence of Rome, by the minister of Baptism—usually a presbyter. In Rome, it was reserved for the bishop, although an earlier anointing at the baptismal site itself was by other ministers. In all cases it was performed in close association with the baptismal act and led at once to admission to Communion. When, in the Middle Ages, the practices of Rome spread throughout Europe where dioceses were large, travel was difficult, and bishops were often absent, a period of time began to open between Baptism and the bishop's post-baptismal "seal." As a result, Confirmation began to be thought of as a life-stage rite, subsequent to Baptism, and associated with at least minimal teaching and competence for first confession.[2] It was this episcopal rite which the 1549 Prayer Book developed into the occasion for public confession of the faith on the part of an adolescent Christian. The content of the rite itself bears witness to its origin in an earlier time for another purpose. It is an accidentally detached portion of the early baptismal liturgy which, in the later Middle Ages and afterward, was put to a use for which it was not created and which it does not actually express.

The service of 1549 had little time to become familiar before it was replaced by the rite of the Prayer Book of 1552. The rubrical material explaining the function of Confirmation is little changed from the previous book, and the catechism for children is virtually identical. Significant alterations appear in the rite itself. In the prayer for the gift of the Spirit, instead of the rather dramatic "send down from heaven . . . upon them the Holy Ghost," the bishop asks God to "strengthen" the confirmands with the Holy Spirit. The prayer "Sign them, O Lord, and mark them . . ." is dropped, and the formula "N., I sign thee with the sign of the cross and lay my hand upon thee . . . " is replaced by a direction that the bishop "lay his hand upon every child severally" (no signing) and say what is unmistakably a prayer: "Defend, O Lord, this child with thy heavenly grace, that he may continue thine forever, and daily increase in thy Holy Spirit more and more, until he come to thy everlasting kingdom." The concluding prayer and blessing remained unchanged. The force of these changes is to reduce the performative sense that in the rite a new divine gift is conferred. The already present Spirit needs to be "strengthened" and "increased."

Another feature of these first two Prayer Books has particular bearing on Confirmation, but to observe it, account must be taken of the Baptism rites. The 1549 Prayer Book, as already noted, removed the anointing from Confirmation. Thus it is remarkable that an anointing was retained in the rite of Baptism, immediately following the Baptism itself. There are not, in the 1549 Book (as there had been in Roman-derived liturgies for several centuries) two initiatory anointings — one by a priest at the Baptism, the other by a bishop, usually at a later time. There was one, and it came in the baptismal rite. The 1552 Book did not continue this anointing; but, like the first Prayer Book, it brought into the baptismal rite material that had been associated with Confirmation. For clarity and economy, the 1552 Baptism service omitted rites which in 1549 had been conducted at the church door. Certain themes and features of the two portions of the baptismal liturgy duplicated one another; so the whole action was brought to the font. But significantly an important part of the omitted material was retained and moved to a post-baptismal location. In the 1549 rite, while at the entry of the church, the child to be baptized was signed with the cross. Addressing the child, the minister explained that the action was "a token that thou shalt not be ashamed to confess thy faith in Christ crucified, and manfully to fight under his banner against sin, the world and the devil, and to continue his faithful soldier and servant unto thy life's end." In the revision of 1552 the consignation was relocated immediately after the Baptism itself, and the charge to the person signed was changed to a statement concerning the intention of Baptism: "We receive this child into the congregation of Christ's flock, and do sign him with the sign of the cross, in token that hereafter he shall not be ashamed to confess the faith of Christ crucified, . . . " The important thing to observe in this relocation is that the images of this passage — the confession of Christ, and strength for combat in the world — were images which the medieval church had associated distinctively with Confirmation. Thus while in 1552, one of the actions, the sign of the cross, was removed from Confirmation, it was retained as a post-baptismal action, where it was interpreted by terms which carried unmistakable associations, not with Baptism, but with Confirmation.

Cranmer knew the patristic liturgical sources available in the sixteenth century, and he would have resisted the efforts of some Reformed authorities to set the New Testament against the early church. It seems likely that we have here an effort on the part of the sixteenth century Anglican reformers to return certain Confirmation actions and interpreting motifs to a location immediately after Baptism, thus restoring portions of the unity of Baptism and Confirmation. To be sure, the Prayer Book pattern followed infant Baptism by the later childhood rite which retained the Western name "Confirmation" and was made a pre-requisite for Holy Communion. Thus the duplications and confusions in the Western medieval initiatory rites were not cleared up by the Prayer Book. The founders of the Anglican liturgical tradition seem to have been aware of the disintegration of the initiatory moments as they had been known in the early church, and they sought to bring Confirmation actions and meanings back into close association with Baptism.[3]

Making the Tradition Work:
Seventeenth to Nineteenth Centuries

The use of the Prayer Book was interrupted almost as soon as it was begun by the coming to the English throne of Mary Tudor (1553–1558) and the reinstatement of the medieval services and service books. Only when the long reign of Elizabeth I (1558–1603) brought the return of the Prayer Book was the reformed liturgy of the English Church sustained for enough time so that it could begin to shape a style of church life.

The Prayer Book rubrics had directed catechizing. The parish clergy, on Sundays and holy days, "half an hour before Evensong, openly in the church," were diligently to "instruct and examine" the children of the congregation. Responsibility also fell to households: "And all Fathers, Mothers, Masters, and Dames, shall cause their children, servants and apprentices (which have not learned their catechism) to come to the church at the time appointed, and obediently to hear and be ordered by the curate until such time as they have learned all that is here appointed for them to learn." These rubrics were supplemented by canons which provided severe penalties for clergy who neglected catechizing. Such legal measures witness both to the importance attached by the Church of England to a tutored laity and to the difficulty of achieving that result. The English system shared with the churches of the Reformation and the Counter-Reformation a passion for education and religious deepening. Many of the clergy were themselves neither educated nor exemplary, and it was a slow business to raise standards of clerical learning and competence.

At first the Prayer Book catechism seems to have been the principal instrument for catechizing. It was widely replaced by individually prepared aids for instructing the young. One of the most popular of these was the *Catechism* issued in 1570 by Alexander Nowell (1507–1602, appointed Dean of St. Paul's in 1560). Nowell's work went through many editions and continued in use until late in the seventeenth century.[4] In ensuing generations, scores of works were prepared and used to bring persons to maturity of faith.[5]

Some bishops were diligent in confirming – as visitation records from the seventeenth century indicated.[6] But others were neglectful of this pastoral duty. Puritan and sectarian objections to episcopacy and the Prayer Book were too often given force by the carelessness of many clergy. In the disruptions of the Civil War and the Protectorate, episcopal Confirmation lapsed altogether. When episcopacy and the Prayer Book were restored in 1661, the occasion was used to introduce into the Prayer Book a provision for adult Baptism and to add in the Confirmation rite an explicit renewal of baptismal promises by the confirmands.[7]

In the eighteenth and nineteenth centuries, Confirmation was held in varying regard. Among Evangelicals, the rite was valued as bringing to articulateness a personal confession of faith. It was virtually an occasion to seek an inward conversion. High churchmen stressed the sacramental gift of the Spirit, the ancient office of the bishop; and the solemnity of one's being admitted to Communion. But there were careless bishops in whose jurisdictions Confirmations were carried out at best infrequently and perfunctorily. The model for the genuinely pastoral parish visitation and Confirmation is usually credited to Samuel Wilberforce (Bishop of Oxford, 1845–69, and of Winchester, 1869–1873). His own earnestness and reverence made Confirmation a memorable occasion. His standard was widely adopted, and Confirmation quite generally became a serious, impressive event for confirmands and parishes.

In the Church of England in the American colonies, there were no bishops. Confirmation was only available in England. By consent, responsible adults were admitted to Communion without Confirmation. In the conditions which prevailed, the wish stood for the act.[8] When the episcopate was secured for the reorganized Episcopal Church, it was some time before all dioceses had bishops; the bishops were rectors of large parishes; dioceses were large; and travel was difficult. Yet from quite early in the last century it has been taken for granted that bishops will make regular visitations for Confirmation. Perhaps if one name is mentioned in connection with establishing such a norm it should be that of John Henry Hobart, whose brief episcopate set a model for energetic pastoral administration of a diocese.

The expectation of regular episcopal visitations – an expectation whose modernity most Episcopalians do not recognize – depends heavily on the private automobile (as previously it was made possible by railroads and stagecoaches). Somewhat ironically, the conditions by which the liturgical system of episcopal Confirmation might be made to work came into being just as serious questions about the system itself arose.

Modern Issues and Questions

In the late nineteenth and early twentieth centuries some early Christian texts which had not previously been known were discovered, and other familiar documents were more accurately dated. This fuller historical knowledge made it clear that the early church knew "Confirmation," if it knew it at all, only as one post-baptismal moment within the rich, unified Easter baptismal Eucharist. To put the point negatively, the early church had no rite of an episcopal visitation to "complete" the initiation of children baptized in infancy. The peculiar Confirmation practices and understandings of the medieval West — practices and understandings which have influenced Romanism, Protestantism and Anglicanism — have derived from the uses of the dioceses around Rome. The checkered, discontinuous story of Confirmation has been filled out in recent decades.

Even though all informed persons could agree that the rites of initiation had been unified in the early church and became divided, almost by accident, in later centuries in the West, different meanings were attached to that important finding:

Some scholars took very seriously the presence in many early liturgies of two ritual moments: a water Baptism moment and an anointing with oil moment. These were given distinct meanings by some early Christian writers. The water moment was spoken of as negative—a washing from sin, a cleansing of forgiveness. The anointing moment was spoken of as positive—the gift of the Holy Spirit. The two were, of course, within one liturgical event. Now that these two acts and meanings, so necessary to each other and to Christian membership, have become separated, what do they mean? How should one interpret the fact that virtually all Christian bodies practice the first of these, but not all practice the second? Some scholars sought to define different ways in which one is met by the divine life in Baptism and in Confirmation. The language of their theological sources persuaded them that, without episcopal Confirmation, Baptism remains, in some sense, incomplete.

Other scholars emphasized that in ritual and meaning Christian initiation is a Christocentric whole—a whole which centers in Baptism and brings one into Christ and the church. Because this act carries a compressed weight of meaning, it is understandable that the early church would develop the ritual, giving it more complexity than is reported in our earliest sources. But the ceremonies before and after Baptism are explicatory; they add nothing to the reality of the sacrament that is not present in the simplest forms of its enactment. When one post-baptismal gesture becomes separated, it cannot carry distinct, independent, essential meanings. Any meanings it has are baptismal meanings. When it is used separately, it can do no more than restate those baptismal meanings.

The literature of this debate is largely English, quite varied, and of considerable intellectual force. Perhaps two influential titles should be mentioned specifically. The late G. W. H. Lampe in *The Seal of the Spirit* (1951, 2nd ed., rev., 1967) argued that Baptism is itself the "seal." But he finds value (on pastoral rather than historical grounds) in a rite in which those who are baptized as infants ratify their baptismal promises. L.S. Thornton's *Confirmation: Its Place in the Baptismal Mystery* (1954) sought to reply that a spirit-moment (Confirmation) is essential to complete sacramental initiation.

It is chastening, in any consideration of the early history of Confirmation, to realize just how varied the pre- and post-baptismal rites were in the early church and how unreflective the changes in the West have been. The mid-1960s saw the publication of several indispensable studies which make available to students the facts of these matters. J. D. C. Fisher's *Christian Initiation: Baptism in the Medieval West* (1965) tells with thoroughness and conciseness the story of the disintegration in the West of the early baptismal rite. Leonel L. Mitchell (who was a member of the Drafting Committee for the rites of the revised Prayer Book) published his *Baptismal Anointing* (1966) demonstrating the variety of pre- and post-baptismal customs in the early church. E. C. Whitaker's *Documents of the Baptismal Liturgy* (2nd ed., rev., 1970) gives in accessible form the texts of initiatory liturgies from the early period and the Middle Ages. Canon Fisher's *Christian Initiation: The Reformation Period* (1970) provides liturgical documents, excerpts from theological works, and the editor's own introductions, dealing with the treatments of Baptism and of Confirmation in the formative years of the sixteenth century. Research, criticism and publication continue, but the material for understanding the history of Christian initiatory ritual is now in hand in a way it has never been before.

At the same time that issues were arising from scholarship, pastoral questions became important. The two-stage rite of infant Baptism followed by childhood Confirmation had grown up in stable Christendom. It suited a time when Christian communities sought to consolidate themselves within the societies in which they were set. It was supposed that, with adequate nurture, children would grow into Christian faith and values as they grew into their language and cultural inheritance. Infant Baptism celebrated birth into the Christian commonwealth, and later Confirmation marked coming of age. With the rapid secularization of society, the culture will not carry one towards faith, but away. The rituals and customs of Christian initiation are always influenced by the relation in which the Christian community stands to the general population. It is delusional to expect rites which were shaped in the era of Christendom to remain appropriate and effective following the death of Christendom.

The church today obviously needs informed, responsible, courageous adults. Yet its nurturing processes and its initiatory provision concentrate heavily on children. Moreover, in modern industrial society, the stages of growing into adulthood are complex and protracted. The traditional administration of Confirmation—with its endless discussion of "the right age"—seemed to propose one charmed moment which stood for the whole meaning of passing from childhood to adulthood in the life of faith and the faith community. Persons at age eighteen do not feel deeply bound by commitments made at age twelve, and persons at age twenty-four feel free to drop or renegotiate engagements entered at age eighteen. Growing up in today's society is a lengthy and difficult process. Even the shaping of a relatively stable and centered self is likely to involve biographical explorations, detours and contradictions.

These factors suggest the "liturgical dissonance" that has been widely felt in Confirmation. Scholarship had shown that the modern rite had come about through a series of historical accidents, and it had been supplied with a theology only after novel customs had taken hold and the stages by which they had developed had been forgotten. Where the early church's theologies (or perhaps more exactly, its pre-theological images) of "spiritual anointing" or "perfecting of Baptism" were repeated as though they interpreted the modern rite, they were applied to an observance so different from that for which they were created that their retention only complicated things. Moreover, practically, the length and character of the process of coming of age in American society is itself the product of modern conditions. Instead of interpreting and supporting the coming into adulthood, Confirmation had become one moment in the process—virtually something to be gotten through. It ordinarily marks the end of a period of instruction—often the last formally ordered instruction available in a parish. And then, after a brief time of serious communion-going, it has been followed by a drift away from the church. A rite of entry and incorporation has too often been a rite of departure.[9]

The widespread revision of liturgies in the past two decades has given the first opportunity in many generations (perhaps the greatest opportunity since the sixteenth century) to adopt better liturgical rites of initiation, expressing a clearer theology, and suiting better the varied ways of becoming a Christian in today's church-world situation.

Prayer Book Revision

The Standing Liturgical Commission began educative steps towards Prayer Book change with the series of "Prayer Book Studies," of which Number I (1950) was *Baptism and Confirmation*. The modestly revised text for Confirmation supplied a smooth liturgical introduction—a thing which the Prayer Book rite notably lacked. The renewal of baptismal vows was made to correspond with the actual promises in the Baptism service. The bishop's prayer for the confirmands, "Send into their hearts . . . the Holy Spirit," suggests a return to the 1549 emphasis on God's acting in Confirmation. After some consideration, the use of chrism was rejected. In 1950, there was, of course, no Trial Use provision, and this study was intended only to stimulate discussion.

The Lambeth Conference of 1968 addressed Confirmation and First Communion briefly. It proceeded on the doubtful basis of seeking a form of commissioning for the laity. (Baptism is the fundamental commissioning of every Christian.) But it proposed two lines of experiment. One was that baptised children be admitted to Communion at a quite early age, Confirmation being postponed until it would be a sign of one's assuming responsibilities of unmistakably adult character. The second would make Confirmation a part of Baptism (including infant Baptism), and admission to the Holy Communion would follow, while the bishop would commission for service at a later life-stage. These suggestions indicated a willingness on the part of Anglican leadership to entertain alternatives to well-established patterns.

After an amendment to the church's Constitution (which passed its final reading in 1967) made it possible for the Episcopal Church to adopt trial rites for use alongside those of the Prayer Book, the Liturgical Commission appointed a Drafting Committee to work on the rites of Christian initiation. The Commission published Prayer Book Studies 18, *Holy Baptism With the Laying-on-of-Hands*, in 1970. A brief introduction outlined the liturgical and pastoral issues to which the rite is addressed. The rite itself is meant for the chief congregational service on Sunday morning. After an opening and a service of the Word with three lessons and a sermon, the candidates are presented; they make (or their sponsors make) brief promises, one summary renunciation, and they reply to the creed in interrogatory form. After a short litany and the blessing of the water, each candidate is baptized. Then "the Bishop or in his absence the priest" prays for the gifts of the Spirit, lays his hand on the head of each one, making the sign of the cross on the forehead, and saying, "N., you are sealed by the Holy Spirit." The persons are received publicly; the peace is exchanged; and the rite continues with the Eucharist at which those who have been baptized may receive. In this rite, the post-baptismal seal (administered by a bishop or a priest) is Confirmation. The life of faith, whose beginning is here signified, is meant to be sustained through participation in the faith community and by the moments of renewal provided by the Eucharist and by active sharing in the liturgy when other persons are baptized.[10]

Some thought was given early in the revision process to the preparation of some "rites of passage" to interpret and support life stages and crises. Some of these were to be for growing children; but beyond that, they would have in mind the entire life-span; and all would be non-initiatory—moments within the biography of a baptized, communicating Christian. But convincing ritual grows organically in a society. In a church and a culture in which authoritative, meaning-bearing "rites of passage" have largely disappeared, it is impossible to devise them at a stroke. Thus, at this point in Prayer Book revision, the formal "ratification" of baptismal vows by children growing to maturity was simply removed as a stage of sacramental initiation. (It always was duplicative for one baptized as an adult.) And nothing was put in its place.

When the initiatory material was included in Services for Trial Use (1971), a Baptism was located early in the book, indicating its foundational place. Although the text was that of Prayer Book Studies 18, the authorizing Convention set down guidelines for its use. The "baptismal section" could be used as the equivalent of the Prayer Book rite of ministration of Holy Baptism, but the full rite was only to be used when a bishop officiated, and then it was not to be used for "children under the present age normal for Confirmation." (An important provision was included in the authorizing resolution allowing baptized children to be "admitted to Holy Communion before Confirmation, subject to the discretion and guidance of the Ordinary." Thus episcopal Confirmation was no longer a necessary requirement for Holy Communion; Christian persons were recognized as sacramentally eligible for the eucharist by reason of Baptism.)[11] This action of the General Convention had the effect of allowing the Liturgical Commission's proposed rite to serve as a revision of the baptismal liturgy while refusing the Commission's fundamental effort to have a complex, unified rite of Baptism-with-the-laying-on-of-hands stand as complete initiation. The daring move from a sacramental/catechetical two-stage rite to a sacramental one-stage rite was rejected. A second stage—a "ratifying" of baptismal promises with episcopal laying-on-of-hands—was to be sustained. Even with all of its anomalies (especially for one baptized as an adult), a catechetical act of "ratification" had a deep grip on the church. Nevertheless, the revision process was well-served by this radical—but at the same time historically deeply conservative—proposal.

Following the publication of *Services for Trial Use*, much consideration was given to Christian initiation at meetings of bishops, the Liturgical Commission, and others. One result was a concise "Statement of Agreed Positions."[12] This statement affirmed the centrality and completeness of Baptism. It contended for the desirability of the baptismal liturgy containing (in addition to Baptism by water and the triune name) "the laying-on of hands, consignation (with or without chrism), prayer for the gift of the Holy Spirit, reception by the Christian community, joining the eucharistic fellowship, and commissioning for Christian mission." Later portions of this statement clarify some important matters: Baptism is theologically, sacramentally, ritually complete Christian initiation. Hence no subsequent rite should be thought of as "completing" it (as though something essential needed to be supplied); and no subsequent rite should be required for admission to the Eucharist. (Receiving Communion is one of the rights and privileges of the baptized.) A bishop who is present at a Baptism presides, but when no bishop is present, Christian initiation in its entirety (including the post-baptismal laying-on of hands) is performed by the officiating presbyter.

The agreed positions go on to speak of "a post-baptismal affirmation of vows." If Baptism is complete, it is complete as an inaugural event which looks to the future. Its completeness needs to be drawn on, and its promises need to be restated. One "pastorally and spiritually desirable" occasion for such an affirmation is when a person baptized in infancy accepts for herself or himself the pledges of Christian faith and life. The statement remarks that such an act must be voluntary, even though it may be sought or expected. A bishop is designated the appropriate minister to receive the affirmations and transmit his blessing. This rite is spoken of as "Confirmation." (This action which fills out what might be thought of as the psychological inadequacy of infant Baptism is the only place in which these "agreed principles" speak of "Confirmation" at all.) The renewal of baptismal promises is, however, in itself an act suitable for marking other occasions within Christian experience. The statement suggests two (neither of which, to repeat, is termed "Confirmation"): the decision of a person baptized in another Christian fellowship to live out the joys and obligations of that Baptism within the Episcopal Church, and a time of return to Christian faith and practice after a period of lapse.

These principles express a direction that is embodied in the next revised initiatory rite: Prayer Book Studies 26. This study was published in 1973 with a Supplement, by the present writer, providing an extended historical, theological and pastoral rationale.

Prayer Book Studies 26 contained (with substantial amending) the design of the baptismal rite of Prayer Book Studies 18. A service of the Word leads to the presentation of the candidates, the renunciations and promises, the blessing of the font, the Baptism, the post-baptismal laying-on of hands (with chrism, if desired) by the bishop, if present, otherwise by the presbyter, the welcome by the congregation, followed by the peace and the Eucharist.[13]

But this rite included the "affirmation of baptismal vows." Members of the congregation routinely join in the promises and thus renew their own baptismal covenant. But provision was made, on an occasion when a bishop is present, for already baptized persons to use this renewal for important non-routinized moments in the life of faith. Moreover, once this reaffirmation is not regarded as initiatory, but as an act within the life of a fully admitted Christian, there is no reason why it may not be done more than once. Thus the reaffirmation of the vows of Baptism is freed to develop as a ritual means for interpreting, supporting and celebrating an indefinite number of moments within the experience of a baptized Christian.

This rite (with some significant political misadventures) became, in essential structural features, the rite of *Authorized Services*, 1973, the *Proposed Book of Common Prayer*, 1976, and of the Prayer Book as adopted in 1979.

The Rite of the 1979 Prayer Book

It will be useful to keep in mind a distinction (implicit in the foregoing narrative) which informs the handling of Confirmation in this revision of the Prayer Book. Confirmation, as we have inherited it in the Episcopal Church, has a complex liturgical history in which two major strands can be distinguished:

1. One component is (a) the sacramental rite—a part of the church's essential ministration of the redemptive life. This element (b) speaks of the Holy Spirit. As such (c) it emphasizes what God does. It is (d) initiatory—one of the signs of becoming a Christian. Since it is a fragment of the early baptismal liturgy, it (e) is properly unrepeatable. This aspect of the Confirmation heritage (f) comes to us from the early church, by way of Rome (where it was kept an episcopal prerogative, contrary to the practice elsewhere) and the medieval West.

2. The other major component is (a) a catechetical rite—speaking of competence and responsibility. Its substance is (b) the ratification of baptismal promises. It therefore emphasises (c) what we do in the stewardship of faith and life. Rather than being initiatory, it (d) belongs within the baptized life; otherwise one has no baptismal promises to renew. There is no reason why, if reaffirming baptismal promises is a

good thing for a Christian to do, it (e) may not be done any number of times. This understanding of Confirmation (f) came to us largely from the sixteenth century, although late medieval developments had prepared for it.

These two features had been combined in the Confirmation service of English and American Prayer Books since 1662.[14] In the 1928 Prayer Book, the catechetical element came first; it appears in the questions and answers at the lower half of p. 296 and the top of p. 297. The sacramental element is represented by the bishop's prayer and laying-on of hands which follow on p. 297. Neither is very fully developed.

The two can seem to have some complementarity. But they originate in different historical settings, and they draw on different conceptualities and literatures. Educators (who are likely to think of the catechetical rite as what Confirmation *really* is) refer to developmental studies such as Gesell, Erikson or Kohlberg. Sacramental theologians and liturgiologists (who usually think that the sacramental rite is what Confirmation *really* is) refer to Hippolytus and other church fathers and discuss the book of Acts. Comprehensive works on Confirmation tend to begin with historical, exegetical and theological chapters which focus on the sacramental rite and say much about the Holy Spirit. Then in later chapters about the age for Confirmation and the preparation of confirmands, the focus shifts markedly to the catechetical rite and the psychology of maturation. The shift usually goes unremarked.[15]

Persons who think in terms of the sacramental aspects tend to want children confirmed at an early age so as to bring Confirmation into close association with Baptism (where alone it is intelligible) and to admit children to the Eucharist at a younger age. Persons who think in educational terms tend to want Confirmation later than it has customarily been so that account can be taken of the protracted stages of adolescence and youth in today's society. Where the conflict between these two tendencies results in early admission to Communion followed by later (sometimes much later) Confirmation, the integrity of the sacramental sequence (Baptism, Confirmation, Communion) is lost.

The most conspicuous feature of the 1979 Prayer Book is that these two clusters of meaning are not treated as two aspects of a single thing, but as two different things. Both are retained, but they are separated and dealt with in different ways.

The sacramental sealing is incorporated in (or, if one is historically minded, it is restored to) the Baptism rite itself. Immediately after the Baptism(s), there is a prayer which begins as thanksgiving for Baptism but turns to a request for the gifts of the Spirit. This prayer is, of course, a revision of the bishop's prayer which stood in the Confirmation rite of the 1928 Prayer Book and its predecessors. It is at least as old as our earliest known baptismal liturgy, *The Apostolic Tradition* of Hippolytus (c. 215 AD), where it comes after the Baptism and before the post-baptismal anointing which is usually taken to be the ancestor of Western Confirmation. The list of gifts of the Spirit in the prayer is based on the qualities of character which are promised in Isaiah 11:2 for an ideal coming king and are here asked as the inner resource for every Christian.

The prayer is followed by the ritual action of the laying-on-of-hands (in which chrism may be used). By the time of the modern revision, the use of chrism by bishops at Confirmation had become fairly widespread, apart from any rubric allowing or suggesting it. There was apparently much acceptance of the custom and little feeling that it should be forbidden. The matter had largely ceased to be divisive. But the imposition of hands had been the authorized gesture of Confirmation in Anglicanism since the sixteenth century, and it was not the intention of the revisers to overset that tradition by requiring anointing. In this Prayer Book, the use of chrism is recognized for the first time, but it is optional.

Accompanying the action is the declaration: "N., you are sealed by the Holy Spirit in Baptism and marked as Christ's own for ever." Although they are associated with the act of laying-on-of-hands, these words refer to the sealing of the Holy Spirit *in Baptism*.[16] This wording can raise a difficulty. If one thinks of the term "Baptism" as referring narrowly to the water action, and of the "seal" as referring to the subsequent laying-on-of-hands, these words which associate the seal of the Spirit with the former action make one wonder why the later action is called for at all. But the words are not to be taken in these overly specific senses. The term "Baptism" can (on ancient and authoritative precedent) refer broadly to a complex action which as a whole is an effective sign of the forgiveness of sin, union with Christ and the church, and the gift of the Spirit. That is the sense that the term "Baptism" is meant to carry here. The Prayer Book is not interested in distinguishing a water-moment and a laying-on-of-hands moment (which are now closely associated in time) and defining certain initiatory meanings as attaching to one and not to the other. That could seem like more of the sacramental and liturgical legalism which has bedevilled Western discussion of Baptism and Confirmation for centuries. Rather, all is Baptism; all is seal. Meanings interpenetrate, for they speak of the unitary life of God which is joined to the unitary life of one of us in a complex, but coherent and unified, liturgical action.

Both the prayer for the Spirit and the laying-on-of-hands are the ministry of a bishop if a bishop is present; otherwise they are done by the officiating presbyter. The intention of the rite is that anyone baptized using this liturgy is, in sacramental terms, baptized, confirmed (in the initiatory sense), and a communicant. In the case of either an infant or an adult, baptism is an act of beginnings, whose validation will only follow after it. But the sacramental act is complete Christian initiation. Late stages of revision and adoption obscured this point somewhat, and, as yet, neither canons nor the yearly report forms which parish clergy must fill out have taken account of redefinition which this liturgical change should entail.

The ratification of baptismal promises—the catechetical rite, to which we now turn—has been handled in a way that differs from previous Prayer Books. We cannot look to the early church for model, for there is only scanty, varied and largely inapplicable information as to what it did with children of believing parents. The early church's Baptism centered normatively on adults who were converts from Hellenistic religions and had several years of prior catechetical training. Their renunciations and promises were conscious and informed. Those ingredients of articulate faith, catechetical instruction and personal commitment which had, in the early church, been integral in Baptism itself (and which are still so for persons baptized in adulthood) had come, in the West, to gather around a second initiatory moment, the moment of adolescent confirmation. Despite the liturgical anomalies, the opportunity for manipulative use of people, and the doubtful results to which the two-stage pattern led, its inclusion of the conscious participation of each Christian in the normal expectation for Christian membership needs to be taken seriously. The church is a community of shared meaning. It is summoned into being in response to proclamation, and it is built up by shared intelligible discourse. It is to be a people of disciplined life, witness and service. When persons baptized as infants are in mind, some form of articulate response seems a proper complement of the baptismal gift.

Yet a single, unrepeated act of ratification, made ordinarily at adolescence, hardly seems to give adequate expression to so profound an impulse. No matter how firmly the pastoral structures of the church may encourage persons who have been baptized as children to reaffirm their baptismal promises for themselves, old motivations have been breaking down. Once the link with First Communion had been set aside, no sacramental privilege hinged on an act of ratification. As a consequence, adolescent ratification of infant Baptism seems to be becoming less regimented. (No longer all of the fifth graders every year!) The point is not, of course, that under new rites and new community dynamics the church should do less than it had under the old. Rather, given what we know about life-stages, there are other occasions—differing from person to person—through our adult Christian experience in which public reaffirmation of one's baptismal vows and the receiving of episcopal

THE LITURGICS OF CONFIRMATION

blessing might be sought. What is needed is not so much catechized children as a catechumenal church. The Prayer Book of 1979 opens such possibilities by making the reaffirmation of baptismal vows a repeatable act.

At an early stage of thinking out this rite, it was the wish of the drafting committee (if the memory of one member is still intact) that the term "Confirmation" be discontinued. It is neither ancient nor universal. And now that the two elements which had combined in "Confirmation" were being separated, it seemed that neither should retain the name. All of the adults who, for whatever reasons, came before the bishop were regarded as doing the same thing: reaffirming the pledges of their Baptism and seeking the blessing of God and the support of the church as they did so. Yet the first printed edition of "Prayer Book Studies 26" introduced the term, at least *sotto voce*, when its subtitle contained the words "The Affirmation of Baptismal Vows, Also Called Confirmation."

Since the rite was essentially repeatable, there seemed no reason why the first occasion of affirming one's baptismal vows should have a different name from later occasions. Nor, in the 1973 text, was there any distinguishing gesture; all received the laying-on-of-hands. But in successive revisions, the title "Confirmation" gained greater prominence, and the idea that it was one form of reaffirming the promises of Baptism became obscured.[17] Moreover, starting with a text issued in 1975, those presented to the bishop were identified in three categories: Confirmation, reception and reaffirmation. This distinction remains in the completed Prayer Book, 1979. A rubric on page 412 gives "Confirmation" the specific sense of the occasion on which persons who had been baptized at an early age, after due preparation, "make a mature public affirmation of their faith and commitment to the responsibilities of their baptism."

The Confirmation liturgy, in the normative form in which it is set forth in the Prayer Book, is part of a unified whole,[18] all of it under the general presidency of the bishop. It begins with a service of the Word, at which the bishop preaches. Candidates for Baptism are presented; then after the renunciations, those persons whose Confirmation, reception or reaffirmation will later be recognized are presented to the bishop by sponsors. In the promises which follow, all in the congregation join. At the Baptism the bishop voices the prayer for the Spirit and lays his hand on each of the newly baptized, saying, "You are sealed . . ." The newly baptized Christians are welcomed by the congregation. Then they, with their sponsors, retire from the focal point of the room, and other persons come before the bishop for Confirmation, or reception, or reaffirmation. The actions of grace which are celebrated here are often of great significance not only to the individuals involved, but also to the parish. This liturgical event makes apprehensible the stir of the Spirit in the church. The Prayer Book directions are minimal. Bishops can and do carry off these varied and humanly rich events with appropriateness and a pastoral flair. The bishop is to lay his hand on the head of each person being confirmed. (No ritual gesture is required, or suggested, or forbidden for "reception" or "reaffirmation".) For the prayer at Confirmation, there are two choices: one is worded around the idea of strengthening; the other is the familiar "Defend, O Lord . . ." When the persons being confirmed (as well as those being received and making reaffirmations) have been dealt with appropriately, the peace is exchanged throughout the congregation, and the liturgy continues with the Eucharist, at which the bishop presides.

In certain respects, this rite marks a break with the Prayer Book tradition. Misgivings over liturgical authority, loyalty to tradition, and bond with other Anglican churches may come to mind. But it is easy to exaggerate discontinuities. Responsible change, in a continuous, living heritage, must put those who undertake it in touch with times of origins. The work of revising initiatory rites has coincided with a fresh examination of sources. The material sketched earlier in this chapter suggests that the Edwardean Prayer Books were seeking to emphasize the completeness of Baptism by bringing sacramental Confirmation into the total baptismal complex of signs. The historical evidence also suggests that Cranmer thought of Confirmation as an important occasion for ratifying the promises of Baptism before the bishop and receiving the "increase" of a Spirit already given in Baptism. In the light of history and theology, it seems no less possible than in the sixteenth century to defend these general intentions. If these were the aims of the Prayer Book tradition, they would seem to be carried out more adequately and clearly in the Prayer Book of 1979 than they were in either of the Books that came from Cranmer's hands.[19]

But the confusion in the Western inheritance of Baptism and Confirmation is very great, and changes in accustomed ways of perceiving and acting make their way slowly. So both in the mid-sixteenth and the late-twentieth centuries the currents and crosscurrents of opinion in the church pretty well assure that the clarity of Anglican Confirmation liturgies will be flawed.

Meanwhile some very considerable gains can be noted.[20] The baptismal rite—now far richer than it has been in previous Prayer Books—includes the action of "the seal of the Spirit." (This ancient initiatory action had, in the life of a baptized person, long been separated from its associated rites by a dozen years or so.) The renewal of the covenant of Baptism is now a repeatable resource. One reaffirms the promises of Baptism routinely at the Easter Vigil or when attending the Baptism of someone else. Implicitly every Eucharist is a renewal of Baptism. But in non-routinized ways, the fundamental pledges of faith and life can now be renewed at occasions of return or rededication which may well mark the lifetime of any baptized person.

Thus, Confirmation (in the specific terms of the Prayer Book) ought to be—in the pastoral structures of the church and the growing experience of Christian young persons—an occasion for "mature, public affirmation of the faith" on the part of those who were baptized as children. But that is not the only or the last time for such an affirmation. Confirmation will ask the church's young people to do—solemnly, before the bishop— what the church's adults do or stand ready to do, as occasions in their lives suggest its appropriateness. This act of reaffirmation, by its repeatability, does not stand as a mark of the separateness of the generations, but of their unity and mutuality in the growing life of faith.

Christian Initiation, Rites of Passage, and Confirmation

Leonel L. Mitchell

"The term initiation," according to Mircea Eliade, "denotes a body of rites and oral teachings whose purpose is to produce a decisive alteration in the religious and social status of the person being initiated." He goes on to describe initiation as a basic change in existential condition. "The novice," he writes, "emerges from his ordeal endowed with a totally different being from that which he possessed before his initiation; he has become *another*."[1] We may arrive at a working definition of Christian initiation by examining this general definition in the light of such scriptural statements as St. Paul's, "I have been crucified with Christ,"[2] or, "If anyone is in Christ, he is a new creation,"[3] or the more communitarian phrase of I Peter, "Once you were no people, but now you are God's people."[4]

We may speak of Christian initiation as that body of rites and oral teachings which make a person a new creation in Christ, a member of the new people of God. This status is further described by Paul in Romans 6 as being buried with Christ in his death so that we may rise with him to new life and by John 3 as being born anew of water and the Spirit; while I Peter declares us to be

"a chosen generation, a royal priesthood, a holy nation, God's own people, that you may declare the wonderful deeds of him who called you out of darkness into his own marvelous light."[5]

With these affirmations we may compare a further description Eliade gives of initiation:

"Initiatory death is indispensable for the beginning of spiritual life. Its function must be understood in relation to what it prepares: birth to a higher mode of being . . . This birth requires rites instituted by the Supernatural Beings; here it is a divine work, created by the will and power of those Beings; it belongs not to nature (in the modern secularized sense of the term), but to sacred history."[6]

This description is clearly consistent with the opening statement of the Roman Catholic general introduction to the rites of Christian initiation:

"Through the sacraments of Christian initiation men and women are freed from the power of darkness. With Christ they die, and are buried and rise again. They receive the Spirit of adoption which makes them God's sons and daughters and, with the entire people of God, they celebrate the memorial of the Lord's death and resurrection"[7]

This same understanding of Christian rites is reflected in two answers from "An Outline of Faith," the catechism in *The Book of Common Prayer*:

"Holy Baptism is the sacrament by which God adopts us as his children and makes us members of Christ's Body, the Church, and inheritors of the kingdom of God."

and

"The inward and spiritual grace in Baptism is union with Christ in his death and resurrection, birth into God's family the Church, forgiveness of sins, and new life in the Holy Spirit."[8]

Common initiatory themes are here expressed in terms of Christian practice, and the appropriateness of the term Christian initiation becomes so evident as to raise the question of whether Eliade and other historians of religion have not drawn their general definitions in the light of their own experience with Christian rites. Certainly Odo Casel, the theologian of the *Mysterienlehre*, has been accused of reading Christian theological concepts into the pagan mystery cults.

Prescinding from the question of the inner meaning of non-Christian rites to those who celebrate them, we may notice the similarity of purpose and structure between the rites of Christian initiation and the initiatory rituals of other religions. Arnold van Gennep, in his classic study of cultural celebrations, *Les rites de passage*, provided convenient categories by means of which to make a more detailed study of those celebrations he called rites of passage, which include those celebrated at an individual's "life crises."[9] Van Gennep analyzed the structure of these rites as consisting of a rite of separation from the former status, a liminal or transitional period, and finally a rite of incorporation into the new status which reintegrated the initiate into the community. He also recognized the possibility that each part of the rite might itself have such a threefold structure.

If we apply van Gennep's categories to traditional Christian rites such as those of *The Apostolic Tradition* of Hippolytus,[10] or those described by Ambrose of Milan [11] or Cyril of Jerusalem[12] in the fourth century, we find that all consist of a rite of separation from the pagan world, admission to the catechumenate, followed by the liminal period of the catechumenate itself, and concluding with the sacraments of initiation which incorporate the neophyte into the *ecclesia*, the Christian community, in the new status of *fidelis*, or as we prosaically describe it, "communicant member in good standing." The concluding rite itself is susceptible to the same tripartite division. The renunciation of the devil is the rite of separation from the old life of sin; the passing through the baptismal waters is the liminal act signifying the movement from one status to the new one; while the signing and sealing of the neophyte, the exchange of the peace, and the reception of Communion are rites of incorporation which incorporate the new Christian into the new role by doing acts characteristic of that role in the liturgy.

The Roman Catholic Rite of Christian initiation of adults has consciously set out to restore, revive and renew this structure in the contemporary church.[13] In that rite Confirmation immediately follows the baptismal washing. The celebrating priest or bishop recites a prayer for the sevenfold gift of the Spirit and makes the sign of the cross on the forehead of the neophyte saying, "N., be sealed with the gift of the Holy Spirit," and greets the newly initiated member with the peace.[14] In the rite of the Episcopal Church the structure for the initiation of adults can be identical. *The Book of Occasional Services* provides traditional forms for the "Preparation of Adults for Holy Baptism,"[15] and in the case of the climactic rite of incorporation, the structure is identical to both the classic rites of the early church and the restored Roman Catholic rite: the candidate renounces the devil (rite of separation) and affirms belief in Christ, passes through the baptismal waters (transitional or liminal rite), is signed on the forehead with the cross with the formula "N., you are sealed by the Holy Spirit in Baptism and marked as Christ's own for ever," greeted with the peace, and admitted to the Eucharist (rite of incorporation).[16] What is different is the terminology employed by the Episcopal Church. The rite of consignation is specifically not called Confirmation, as it is in the Roman Catholic Church.

Not only does the rite of *The Book of Common Prayer* have the same structure as the classical Christian rites of initiation, the rubrics straightforwardly declare that it is the complete rite:

"Holy Baptism is full initiation by water and the Holy Spirit into Christ's Body the Church."[17]

This naturally raises the question of the place of Confirmation as an initiatory rite in the Episcopal Church. As we have seen, Confirmation is traditionally considered one of the "sacraments of initiation" forming with Baptism and First Communion the final climactic act of the initiation process. But in fact this traditional scheme has long been disused and its restoration today is nowhere complete. The actual form of Christian initiation with which most of us are familiar has a very different structure, a structure which developed in the late Middle Ages and became normal, if not normative, for most churches at the time of the Reformation.[18] In this structure Baptism is not administered at the end of a long catechumenate as the "rite of incorporation" but as soon as possible after birth. It marks the beginning rather than the end of the initiation process. The liminal state is several years in duration and is marked by various forms of Christian education or catechetics culminating in early adolescence with Confirmation, commonly called "joining the Church," and admission to Holy Communion.

In this structure Confirmation becomes the climactic and determinative rite. Everyone, or almost everyone, is baptized, but only those who intend to participate actively in the church are confirmed. At least, this would be the situation if the candidates for Confirmation and First Communion chose freely to participate in these rites. In practice many things militate against this happening, although even under ideal circumstances this pattern has serious weaknesses. It functioned best in closely-knit Christian societies, such as the villages of medieval Europe or of Tudor and Stuart England. Christian education was a part of general education and Christian practice a part of good citizenship. The terms communicant and citizen were practically synonyms, and Confirmation and First Communion marked the important societal transition from child to adult. The pattern proved sufficiently viable and stable to survive the Reformation and avoid serious challenge until the disruption of village life caused by the Industrial Revolution.

On the negative side, young people were under tremendous social pressure to conform. To refuse to be confirmed was to refuse to take one's place in society, and simple conformity rather than religious conviction might easily be the end result. In our contemporary situation many of those baptized are not confirmed. Many receive no Christian nurture at all after their Baptism and even of those who do many are never presented for Confirmation. Popularly Confirmation is viewed as a denominational rite identifying the confirmand with a particular religious body, such as the Episcopal Church. This almost necessarily results in the privatization of religion as one of a number of options for the maturing person. It does not, however, necessarily mean that those who are confirmed are committed to being Episcopalians, or even Christians, and Confirmation is often jokingly described as the rite of exit from the Episcopal Church.

Most obviously, various forms of peer and parental pressure prevent the young people who are the usual candidates for Confirmation today from making a free individual choice. The Prayer Book speaks of a "mature public affirmation of their faith and commitment to the responsibilities of their Baptism,"[19] but the inherited structure makes it difficult for this to happen. Where parish custom decrees that children are confirmed in the sixth or eighth grade, or at any other fixed time, it may be psychologically impossible for young people to resist being confirmed along with their classmates. If membership in the church is important to their parents, whether through religious conviction or their own desire to identify with a particular group of actual or potential peers, the children may feel compelled to conform. If Confirmation also takes place at the time in the lives of young people when they are beginning to feel most resentful of parental authority and desirous of becoming their own persons, or immediately before the onset of this adolescent rebellion, the church will be identified by the confirmands with the childish things they wish to put away in their quest for adulthood. Frequently, there is substantial resentment directed against the church for its part in this process. Alternatively, the young people may be confirmed quite willingly, with eager devotion, only to lose interest in the church as their attention turns to other concerns, such as awakening sexuality, or even to altruistic goals such as the elimination of world hunger or nuclear disarmament. In either case, a sharp decline in church-related activity by those recently confirmed is frequently observed.

Confirmation is presented to young people as a rite of passage which will alter their status from that of children to adults in the Christian community. Confirmation, or more probably admission to Communion, may have fulfilled that role in the village societies we have previously mentioned, in which admission to Communion was a significant social event for the entire community, and in which the communicants were treated and permitted to function as adults, but it does not and cannot function this way in contemporary American society. Young people either know or suspect that this is the case. A distinguished Roman Catholic theologian told me that as a boy he knew the nun was lying when she told him that his First Communion was the most important event of his life, since that place had already been preempted by catching his first trout. Since the church does not occupy the central place in the life of our society, nor even of most of those who attend it, there is no church-centered rite which can effectively mark the transition from child to adult in our culture. It has been widely suggested that the real puberty rite in America is the receiving of the first driver's license, but even this is an oversimplification, since our culture is really unable to make the transition from child to adult and has invented the category of the "teenagers" to plug the gap, a liminal state which continues from the beginnings of adolescent rebellion until they are transformed into young adults through marriage and a job, often after years of education have moved them well out of the chronological teens.

I would propose agreeing to a great extent with the late Dean Urban Holmes,[20] that the problem is basically neither with the children nor their parents, nor even with American society, but with their understanding of what Confirmation is and what it does. I do not believe that Confirmation is a rite de passage, nor that it can be made to function as one in our culture. Baptism, of course, is the great Christian rite of passage, our transitus with Christ from death to life, and when the term Confirmation is used to describe an integral part of that rite, then it may be included within that term, but this is not what the Episcopal Church understands Confirmation to be. Confirmation is described in the new Catechism as:

> " . . . the rite in which we express a mature commitment to Christ, and receive strength from the Holy Spirit through prayer and the laying on of hands by a bishop."[21]

This is thoroughly consistent with the central prayer of the rite itself which thanks God that "by the sealing of your Holy Spirit you have bound us to your service" in Baptism, and prays, "Renew in these your servants the covenant you made with them at their Baptism."[22] Confirmation is not seen as adding some new grace to that already received, but as renewing and intensifying the grace already given in Baptism.[23] This does not describe a rite of passage. No new status is conferred. It is essentially an individual rather than a social event in which the person embraces a new dimension of the life in Christ. Following Eliot Chapple and Carleton Coon, Urban T. Homes describes this as a rite of intensification.[24]

The 1979 Book of Common Prayer does not, in fact, presuppose the structure which the Episcopal Church inherited from the late Middle Ages. Dean Holmes, Professor Marion Hatchett and I have all argued at length the vexed historical questions concerning the meaning of Confirmation,[25] but there can be little doubt that the present Prayer Book does not see Confirmation as the final act of a process leading to full membership in the church. Full membership is conferred to Baptism. In this it is following traditional Anglican theology, which describes Baptism and the Eucharist as the two sacraments "generally necessary to salvation,"[26] rather than Anglican practice as exemplified in the "Confirmation rubric" of previous editions of the Prayer Book,[27] or the inclusion of the phrase "who have been confirmed by a Bishop of this Church" in the definition of "communicants in good standing" in the Canons of the Episcopal Church.[28]

There seems to be no ground for believing that growth into Christian maturity proceeds in a straight line. People mature at differing rates and to different degrees. Periods of faith and commitment may be followed by periods of doubt and disengagement. It is therefore difficult to be prescriptive about the age and circumstances under which a person should be confirmed. The *Supplement to Prayer Book Studies 26* concluded:

> "The conclusion seems inescapable that in this long, often turbulent transition to adulthood, so many stages are passed through that any single moment for Confirmation is too early to capture some important possible meanings of the process, or too late to express others . . . In the conditions of modern society, no single point can represent the meaning of growing into adulthood."[29]

This recognition led Dean Holmes into a discussion of the repeatability of Confirmation. He argued that rites of intensification can be repeated, and are appropriately repeated as persons come to new and deeper understandings of faith, or emerge from crises of doubt or periods of non-participation. He rejected the distinction made by the Prayer Book between Confirmation and reaffirmation of vows.[30] The fullest statement of this distinction is found in the introduction to *Prayer Book Studies 26*.

> "The occasion of the affirming of baptismal vows and obligations that were made by godparents on one's behalf in infancy is a significant and unrepeatable event. It is one's 'Confirmation Day.' The rite itself, however, is suitable, and should be available, for other occasions in the lives of Christian people . . ."[31]

This distinction is made in the Prayer Book itself by the provision of different formulae for "Confirmation" and "reaffirmation".[32] Of this argument Dean Holmes remarked:

> "I call this the argument from subjective intentionality. It is fraught with all kinds of problems. On the level of personal experience and practice, it is simply untrue . . . On a more theoretical level, the

argument from subjective intentionality commits the basic sociological error of assuming that we can know the subjective intention
of another or even control it . . . The insistence that we must
distinguish between Confirmation and subsequent reaffirmation is
more the result of our own inherited tradition coloring our thought
than anything that can be supported by the data."[33]

Holmes' final point is well made. Anglicanism has always been of at
least two minds as to what Confirmation actually meant. Some have
identified Confirmation with the post-baptismal consignation and the
sevenfold gift of the Spirit, the position most frequently identified with
the name of Dom Gregory Dix,[34] others have seen it as an adult affirmation of baptismal vows by those for whom the vows were made by godparents in infancy, the position usually identified with G. W. H.
Lampe.[35] Often the distinction has not been recognized, and people
have spoken of Confirmation without distinguishing between its senses.
This has resulted in nearly total confusion.

Clearly what Dix described as Confirmation is a part of Baptism in the
1979 *Book of Common Prayer*; the anointing, signing with the cross, and
imposition of a priestly hand which follows the baptismal washing.[36]
Equally clearly, Confirmation in the Prayer Book combines a ratification
of baptismal promises with the laying on of hands and a prayer for increased spiritual growth.[37] As Dean Holmes has ably shown,

"No one spoke of Cranmer's rite as imparting character, until we
found it important to show that the sacramental system had been
perpetuated in its full integrity from Christ until now, an 'integrity'
somewhat uncritically interpreted by late medieval (and early
modern) Roman Catholic theology."[38]

I myself have argued[39] against the use of the word "Confirmation" at all
in the present context, since I believe firmly that it causes unnecessary
difficulties through the lack of agreed-upon definitions, but such an approach has not proved acceptable to the Episcopal Church. We have
therefore retained the use of the word Confirmation to mean a specific act
of "confession of faith": that made for the first time by a person previously baptized, when it is made in the presence of the bishop, who
imposes hands and prays for the spiritual growth of the person making
the profession.

For those baptized in infancy, this act of "Confirmation" is both
theologically significant and pastorally necessary — some would say
theologically necessary as well. It ritualizes the "owning" by the individual of the faith in which he or she was baptized. Holmes' point is
that there is no *real* distinction between this "owning" of faith and the act

of one who returns to faith and accepts it personally, even though the person had been confirmed as well as baptized at an earlier time.

It is even more difficult for me to understand the meaning of Confirmation when it is administered to a person who has been baptized as an adult, making his or her own baptismal promises, unless some spiritually significant event, whether good or bad, stands between that person and the reception of Baptism. There is a theological redundancy in this approach which needs further consideration.

There is an approach, however, from which our practice does make sense. It begins with the assertion of the episcopal nature of the Episcopal Church. Our present practice brings each and every lay member of the Episcopal Church before the bishop, there to affirm personally his or her baptismal covenant. If the person was baptized in the Episcopal Church, this occasion is called Confirmation. If the person was baptized and confirmed in another church, it is called reception. If it follows a period of lapse from Christian faith and practice, it is called reaffirmation. All renew their baptismal vows, "own" their faith, and receive the laying on of episcopal hands. The only exceptions to this policy are those adults who are baptized by the bishop himself, who, of course, make their baptismal vows in his presence and receive the post-baptismal signing and sealing at his hands. The practice is consistent. What is confusing is the terminology. Dean Holmes may well be right that we have made a distinction without a difference, but I believe it is only a verbal distinction.

Confirmation is not intended to be a rite of passage for young people entering into adulthood. It is a rite of intensification, a ritual renewal of the covenant of our Baptism. For Episcopalians the bishop has a prominent and necessary place in this rite. It is, in fact, the necessity of the bishop's ministry which is most widely agreed by Episcopalians to be the essence of Confirmation.

The ritual pattern presupposed by the present rite is that children will be baptized at Easter or another baptismal feast following their birth. They will be reared and nurtured in the Christian community, regularly receiving Communion from an early age, so that they grow to maturity in an environment of Christian love, concern and practice of which they themselves are part. At some appropriate point when they feel ready to own their faith as adults, they will be confirmed. This will entitle them to no new privileges and commit them to no new responsibilities. They will receive at this time, as throughout their life in Christ, the outpouring of the Holy Spirit to enable them to live the baptismal and eucharistic life. Other persons will enter the Christian community as adults (or older children) and will make their own commitment at the time of their Baptism. If this is not done in the presence of the bishop, it will be renewed in his presence so that they may be personally related to their Father in God. The ongoing life of the baptized Christians joining Sunday by Sunday in the Eucharist, and year by year in the Baptism of other Christians intensifies and expands their life in Christ and the Spirit. This is the ideal pattern of *The Book of Common Prayer.*

In practice, many things interfere. Parishes are not always, or even often, the Christian environments for loving nurture which are needed to bring children of all ages to Christ. Customs associated with earlier ritual patterns reassert themselves. A First Communion class for first–graders and a Confirmation class for senior high–schoolers make an appearance. All four orders of ministers allow "the way we've always done it" to usurp the place of real tradition, and nothing much changes from the inherited late medieval pattern. Parents insist that their children receive the same sort of Confirmation instruction as they did and be confirmed at the age of twelve "just like Jesus." Bishops preach Confirmation sermons attributing to that rite effects which properly belong to Baptism. "Thus," as Calvin so aptly phrased it, "a half of the efficacy of Baptism is lopt off."[40] Priests, deacons and religious educators set priorities which have little or nothing to do with helping people "to make a mature public affirmation of their faith and commitment to the responsibilities of their baptism and to receive the laying-on-of-hands by the bishop."[41] This is not really surprising, since Confirmation has been aptly described as a rite in search of a rationale, and throughout Christian history the name has been applied to a variety of actions, including communion from the chalice.

The Episcopal Church, through the *Book of Common Prayer* has opted to make Confirmation a rite presided over by the bishop, at which mature Christians own their baptismal faith. At other times and places it has been used to describe the post-baptismal signing and sealing, and it is so used by many people today. Canon J. D. C. Fisher of the Church of England, for example, has written,

"The reason why Anglicans are reluctant to see very little children confirmed is because they cannot divest their minds of the belief that ratification of vows and some degree of personal commitment are indispensable to Confirmation. Once it is realized that this is not so, the way becomes clear to giving Baptism, Confirmation, and Communion in that order to children of a tender age, and to postponing ratification of vows to an age which is considered pastorally expedient.

"There is a place for a rite of ratification of vows, perhaps with a solemn blessing, at the age when children are able to assume the responsibilities of adult Church membership, provided that such a rite is not regarded as Confirmation, *which is something different.*"[42]

The final phrase indicates clearly that he does not regard as Confirmation the very rite which the American Prayer Book calls Confirmation. This is not the place to debate the theological merits of both positions, but simply to note that what those who agree with Canon Fisher say about Confirmation cannot be applied to the rite in the American Prayer Book, and it is the often unwitting attempt of people to do so which results in the mixed signals being given in the Episcopal Church today. The commentary of Peter Hinchliff is germane:

"In the field of initiation-rites the experts are attempting to reduce the confusion by producing forms which express a coherent understanding of the meaning of Baptism and Confirmation . . . The committee is able to produce a rite which is neat, consistent, and capable of being explained logically. The committee, however, seldom has the power to authorize the use of the rite. Modifications are introduced by those who have that power but not the expertise: the pattern is destroyed once more.[43]

Liturgies, however, are not composed by committees of experts, either in the House of Bishops, the Standing Liturgical Commission, or the Church of England. They are the product of the life of the Church. Episcopalians are clearly not going to abandon their practice of Confirmation. Equally clearly, they are not using it in exactly the way the drafting committee which prepared it expected it to be used. Changes in practice are taking place, at different rates of speed, and often based on different understandings of what is being attempted. It is a simple matter to revise *The Book of Common Prayer* compared to changing the patterns of religious socialization of people and congregations. At the present we can have only insights, suggestions and critiques. A definitive study must await the establishment of new patterns. Liturgical rites may be proposed by the Liturgical Commission and authorized by General Convention, but they do not really become liturgy until they have been chewed, digested, and assimilated by the Christian communities and individuals who use them so that they become a part of their inner being and the basis of their acting and thinking. The "popular" understanding of Confirmation, or of many other rites, is not identical with the sacramental or liturgical theology propounded by "experts." We do not yet know what the popular understanding of the new rites of the 1979 Prayer Book will be. We must recognize, however, that throughout its history Confirmation has proved highly adaptable, changing both form and rationale to meet new cultural or pastoral situations. Perhaps its very lack of a secure and clear biblical and patristic foundation makes it more adaptable than other rites. I do not doubt it will continue to change and adapt itself to the new demands of our contemporary culture.

Aspects of Childhood Confirmation

Iris V. Cully

Historians have traced the development of Confirmation and theologians have explored interpretations. Eventually, pastors and other teachers have to deal with the preparation of people for Confirmation. Many will have to prepare children. This task has been tried in many ways with varying results. This chapter will look at the present situation, develop goals, suggest preparation and explore the meaning of the process.

The Reality

Confirmation is offered children as early as the age of eight in some parishes and it will be assumed that the term "child" pertains until the age of thirteen (or eighth grade). With all the theological assertions involved in the profession of faith, how possibly can a child be given adequate preparation?

One positive aspect is the fact that Confirmation would take place at a time when children are open and trusting in their relationships. If life has been kind to them (and it has not been to some children), they know what it is to love and trust God. They are able to receive this love and to perceive as good the world God has made. This is important because the confirmand is asked to commit life to Christ. We do not commit ourselves to someone we neither know, love, nor trust. Commitment involves the whole person. Adults may have learned how to compartmentalize their lives so that they can separate an intellectual commitment from an emotional commitment. The life of a child is less fragmented. What adults sometimes perceive as simplicity may be genuine wholeness. The child as child can commit life to Jesus Christ. This is different in some ways from the commitment that would be made at the age of sixteen, twenty-five, or sixty, but it is equally important to the individual and valid as a statement of faith.

Children are open to goodness. They have a need to be good and do good. This is encouraged by the tutelage of parents and teachers who are nurturing and teaching them. Children are being fashioned for life in a particular family and community. Usually they receive and conform with some ease to rules that set limits on their behavior. There is security in knowing what brings approval from significant adults. When they are taught that there is a rule of the Christian life, they can understand this in a fairly uncomplicated way.

The positive aspect of "being good" is to do good, to act in ways that show concern for other people. Children begin life concerned about themselves. Through the process of development they learn to transcend the self and consider the needs of other people. Being self-centered seems more comfortable at first, and some adults never outgrow it. Being passively responsive to the demands of others is not unselfishness, either. This indicates a lack of self-regard, the positive self-image essential to becoming fully the self God intended. The ability to "do good" is essential to one seeking Confirmation because each person makes a promise to *follow* Christ. This is the concrete expression of being committed to Christ. It is stated in the baptismal covenant recited between celebrant and people, including the confirmands:

"Will you proclaim by word and example the Good News of God in Christ?

"Will you seek and serve Christ in all persons, loving your neighbor as yourself?

Will you strive for justice and peace among all people, and respect the dignity of every human being?" (BCP, p.305)

The implications of this statement for the preparation for Confirmation will be explored later.

Another reality of Confirmation for children is that the rite marks one point in the process of Christian growth and commitment. For others this point may happen during adolescence, or at any of the "stages" of adulthood. The promises made in Baptism pertain to a person's whole being and are made for all of life. This need not make them overwhelming affirmations for a ten-year-old because each makes a commitment in terms of a particular age and stage in life. Children know about promises. They are beginning to understand openness toward the fulfillment of a promise rather than rigidity in keeping it. The promise to live the Christian life brings responsibilities at this age that would be different at another age, but the integrity of the personal affirmation is equal. The key word is "process." The consistency of individual character assures the continuance of a commitment in some form at each stage of life.

Childhood Confirmation comes at a time when children are still close to the family structure, nurtured in the parental religion, and believing in what they have been taught and see in others. It is easy for them to accept what they hear, to learn what they are taught, to believe what they are told. They are not yet taking cues from a wider peer community, or questioning their religious faith as a result of the diversity they meet at school. This means that they are receiving the rite when secure in their faith. Confirmation is frequently a family matter. The family may even be urging it. Other boys and girls, growing up in similar church families, form the Confirmation class.

There may be value in taking this step before the adolescent quest for identity begins and before the onset of doubt that makes commitment difficult. The assurance of being fully part of the Christian community can impart its own security as the teenager gradually grows away from the "affiliative" family faith toward the uncertainties of searching faith.[1] The possibility remains open for a recommitment in some setting at later stages. The Roman Catholic religious educator Pierre Babin and others have suggested such a rite near the conclusion of adolescence, when young people have achieved a plateau of certainty as they enter upon young adulthood.[2] Whenever a congregation joins confirmands in confessing the creed, these people are making a reaffirmation of faith, but unless they do so with conscious intent, it has little affirming power. There is meaning for the child who makes a confession of faith at this level. The interpretations will deepen across the years, but the intent will remain the same. "Strengthening" is a continuous process. When this aspect of the rite is emphasized, its application to childhood makes sense. The act of Confirmation is a beginning.

However, it is not a rite of passage, despite its once-and-for-all nature. Urban T. Holmes made this clear in his book on the subject.[3] A rite of passage, as anthropology reveals, takes a person from one role and status, separates the person from the community for awhile, and then places the person in a different role and status. Confirmation does not do this. The newly confirmed are not really placed in another category within the Christian community. In practice, there may be so little change that many soon forget that the occasion was supposed to be momentous in any way. There *should* be some difference, and that will be considered later.

Confirmation has more the character of a rite of intensification, that affirms a person in a role, while meeting specific needs for its fulfillment. Confirmation is a rite of sanctification, as its connection with the gift(s) of the Holy Spirit suggests. It has this in common with the Eucharist, which is the primary rite of intensification or strengthening. Confirmation as a rite of strengthening has recently developed a different relationship to the Eucharist than it used to have. It had long been a custom in the Western church to withold participation in the Eucharist until a person was confirmed. The Roman Catholic church changed this practice early in the twentieth century on the basis that the grace conferred by the Holy Communion should be available to children as soon as they reached the age when they could discern right from wrong. Recent liturgical and historical studies brought back the sense of the wholeness of the initiation rite that the Eastern churches never lost because Baptism, Confirmation and Communion are given the infant at one time. Most children being confirmed today in the Episcopal church will already have been admitted to the Lord's Table, so the preparation for Confirmation will not need to include preparation for the Eucharist rite.

This discussion of the situation is not meant as an *apologia* for the Confirmation of young children. I am neutral on the subject. It is an effort to help those who will be preparing children to understand the reality. These boys and girls are at an age of openness and trust, eager to be and do the good deeds that express their trust. Confirmation promises are made with integrity at their own level of growth, and Confirmation itself is a stage in the process of their development as Christians. These children are expressing the religion nurtured by their families and are joining with friends in the experience. Because of these factors of age and family context, later occasions will be needed for the reaffirmation of faith on a different level of understanding and experience.

For the liturgical churches conferring the rite of Confirmation has frequently meant an end to the Christian education of children. This should cause concern because of the possibility either that some will never grow into a mature faith, or that they will soon become dropouts from a community that no longer treats them as children but has no real place for them as full members. The preparation for Confirmation needs to be considered part of the religious education program, and to be followed by education suited to the needs of those who have made a personal confession of faith and have been received into the congregation.

Goals

Without goals people do not know where they are going, and cannot plan their direction. The Confirmation service itself sets the goals for the Christian life in the form of the promises made by the candidates and ratified by the congregation. These are:

(1) reaffirm their renunciation of evil;

(2) renew their commitment to Jesus Christ.

The candidate promises, with God's grace, to follow Christ as Savior and Lord. To these promises are added expressions of what it means to follow Christ:

> Continue in the apostles' teaching and the fellowship, in the breaking of bread, and in the prayers.

> Persevere in resisting evil, and whenever you fall into sin, repent and return to the Lord.

> Proclaim by word and example the Good News of God in Christ.

> Seek and serve Christ in all persons, loving your neighbor as yourself.

> Strive for justice and peace among all people, and respect the dignity of every human being (BCP, pp. 415–17).

The goals of the preparation for Confirmation must have some relationship to those promises. They must help the learner understand the meaning and give some direction for fulfillment.

This cannot be accomplished in six weeks, or in six months. To attempt that would be to trivialize the experience and to suggest that either it can be easily accomplished or that it is so vast a goal that there is no point in trying. No matter how often a group meets, the process of preparation needs to continue at least a year. After a period of weekly meetings, there will still need to be periodic gatherings for reflection and sharing, and at least one individual conference with the pastor/teacher.

The promises from the rite of Confirmation could be grouped under three main goals.

1. *To confess one's personal faith in Jesus Christ as Lord and Savior.* Preparation would include exploring the words "Lord" and "Savior" so as to understand the meaning of these terms; reading the gospel records of who Jesus Christ was and is in order that learners might grow in personal relationship to him, understanding what the phrase "faith *in*" means as seen through New Testament people who confessed Christ, and beginning to express the meaning of that relationship in life.

2. *To live as a Christian.* Preparation must state this promise in terms of the life of a child of eight, ten, or twelve years. This requires insight into the life of a child and includes children's own self-perceptions. They will need to ask how they can live as Christians in their family, school and friendship circles. The preparation would also include

exploring the words and deeds of Jesus as models of how to act in relation to other people, sharing with one another situations in life that affirm Christian living as well as those in which it is difficult to live as Christians. Setting some directions and beginning to practice actions that express God's love and their love for God will be other elements in preparation.

3. *To grow as participant in the life and service of the Christian community.* Acts 2:42, quoted in the promise, is a clue to understanding the meaning in an early Christian community and gives direction for understanding its meaning for the church today. Fulfilling the goal would include cultivating the habit of regular church attendance, growing in the understanding of the liturgy, and beginning to take responsibility in the life of the parish. The parish has the responsibility for providing opportunities. The children will also need to become knowledgeable about how the church is accomplishing its mission around the world.

Preparing for Confirmation: The Pastoral Concern

Readers by now have become aware of the omission of the term "Confirmation instruction." This is deliberate. The general model that priests have followed has been to give information to children, assign material to be learned, and personally interpret such materials. It has usually been assumed that people needed knowledge *about* specific materials in order to be ready for Confirmation. But if Confirmation is a giving of the self to Christ, an affirmation of trust and a commitment of life, no amount of knowledge will either explain the breadth of the decision or be of help in fulfilling the promise. This does not mean that Christians are to be ignorant, but that their knowledge arises out of their continuous search to grasp more fully the meaning of the commitment they make. This cannot be accomplished in advance. The only hope in Confirmation instruction is to set a person's feet on the path. This is the beginning of a pilgrimage. Christians are on a journey.

For this reason, one aspect of the preparation for Confirmation is the pastoral concern. Frequently priests have done what any Sunday School teacher could have done: gone through a course of instruction in the Ten Commandments, Creed, and Lord's Prayer, possibly using the Offices of Instruction. The superior theological education of a cleric was supposed to ensure orthodoxy for the interpretation of these materials. How little we know! No one at any age fully understands the meaning of these words and Christians can only share with one another the meaning in their lives and in the church.

The pastoral aspect of preparation should be designed to help children understand basic Christian statements in a personal way. The pastor, who knows each child, and sometimes has baptized the child earlier, is the best person to guide this spiritual development. Parents and Sunday school teachers have shared their faith. Now, when a new step in the Christian life is about to begin, the pastor has an opportunity to help boys and girls in their growing relationship to God, the life of prayer, and their experience of and participation in Christian worship. The pastor can help them in their struggles to "be good and do good," to understand why it is so difficult to get along with some people, to deal with anxiety, fear, anger, sadness; to increase their understanding of petition, intercession and thanksgiving. Some ten-year-olds still understand sin and forgiveness as it was taught at the age of four. Here, theology meets life, and a concerned pastor can meet needs.

The priest needs to know each child and each family, including families not related to the parish whose children are preparing for Confirmation. For some children (and priests) personal conferences can be awkward; the difference in age and status may preclude any real meeting. Clergy who find it difficult to meet with children should admit this to themselves and work in the preparation for Confirmation with someone, lay or clerical, who can meet this need of personal communication. Sometimes the pastoral concern can be expressed in informal ways. Frequently it will be discerned simply in the way the group meeting is conducted, the interaction and sharing that goes on among members.

This preparatory time could establish a relationship between priest and young communicants so as to develop a positive attitude toward clergy as persons who can help growing Christians in their spiritual journey. This aspect of Confirmation "instruction" has not often been a deliberate focus of preparation.

Preparing for Confirmation: The Educational Concern

This is the area that most people really mean when they talk about preparing for Confirmation: a number of sessions in which children are told what they should know about the Christian faith in order to be ready for the rite. A contrasting view was offered by a commission in the Diocese of New York as long ago as 1962. It reads:

"The stress should be on imparting the joy and wonder of Christianity, for the child should come to know religion as a joyful experience. At the same time no attempt should be made to hide the

Cross and the costliness of discipline and struggle. The child who is learning to love God will make a response in Christian Behavior."[4]

Notice the emphases: joy, wonder, the Cross, costliness, loving God and making a response in behavior. What a vision for the preparation for Confirmation.

As a matter of fact, a few such courses have been published. Chad Walsh's book, *Knock and Enter*,[5] written many years ago, is designed around the experiences within a family setting, as an introduction to the understanding of Bible and doctrine. C. William Sydnor, at that time with the national church's Department of Christian Education, wrote a leader's guide, *Confirmation Instruction for Eleven-to Fourteen-year Olds* in 1965.[6] This was built around an examination of the promises already made in their behalf in Baptism and a study of the promises they will make to the bishop in Confirmation. Various methods are suggested to help young people feel at ease in asking questions, revealing concerns and raising issues. *The Episcopalian*[7] outlined an experience filled with pupil-oriented materials that conveyed the basic understanding of *An Outline of the Faith* (BCP, p. 845) through lively methods. These examples suggest that Confirmation classes should not be designed to make up for suspected deficiencies of the Sunday School. There must be a distinctive focus in order to be effective.

The key is the service of Confirmation itself. Like catechumens since early days, these boys and girls are preparing for a significant event in their lives. They need to study the liturgy in order to understand the meaning of the promises they will make. They may be astonished to realize, when they first read the baptismal service, that someone has already made these promises for them. They are about to make the decision as to whether they are ready and willing to answer for themselves.

The service begins with the renunciation of evil; specifically to renounce Satan and all the spiritual forces of wickedness that rebel against God, the powers of this world, and sinful desires. Such words sound quaint, if not slightly unreal to modern ears. The symbolism and picture language need to be clarified. The Bible is filled with the sense of the struggle between good and evil, and the Resurrection of Christ is discerned as the turning point. The powers of this world both attract and repel, as every child already knows. "Sinful desires" is a term that needs to be understood psychologically as well as theologically, lest it become a source of fear and repression rather than an encouragement to desire the good. Experiences of people, past and present, awareness of the world in which we live, illumine the meaning of the act of renunciation of evil. The Bible, from beginning to end, records this struggle.

The next set of questions points to the relationship of the believer to Christ: to commit oneself to him and to follow him as Savior and Lord. A review of the gospel witness to Christ will help the class probe the meanings of the title "Savior" with reference to the understanding of redemption. (See p. 848, *BCP*); and the title "Lord," with its ancient meanings of fealty, considering how that translates into contemporary meanings for the relationship of the believer to Christ. The candidates will begin the lifelong task of seeking to know what it means to follow Christ personally and as a member of the Christian community.

These questions should be explored beyond their intellectual meanings, although it might be easier to stop there. A promise must be "owned" and its fulfillment becomes part of life. Stories and films about people who have lived obediently to Christ from the earliest times to the present will help young people glimpse a lifestyle that is both fulfilling and dangerous. There are people in any parish who could come to share with the class what this commitment has meant in their lives.

The next basic element in the preparation for Confirmation would be a study of the confession of faith, the Apostles' Creed. The boys and girls may already be acquainted with the Nicene Creed because it is used in the Eucharist. By comparing the two, the likenesses and differences can be established. The first clear difference is that the Nicene Creed is in the "we" form because it was developed by the church in council as a definition of the faith, primarily of the doctrine about Christ. The Apostles' Creed, stated in the first person singular, has roots in the earliest baptismal confessions of faith. You will want the class to look at baptisms recounted in the book of Acts to see the ways in which the confession was stated.

Consideration of the first article of the Creed will suggest biblical passages about God the Creator, as well as present experiences of God's creative work. The second section recapitulates the gospel story. The third section gathers up the work of the Holy Spirit and the basic affirmations of Christian faith.

A variety of methods may be used to bring out the living quality of the Creed. Remember that Christians are affirming their faith *in* God, not faith *about* God. It is not an intellectual statement, although it has content, but primarily a confession. From this follow two corollaries. First, it is not in the Anglican tradition to insist on any one interpretation as final. Freedom of interpretation within the community of faith is acceptable. Secondly, whatever present meaning the words may have for boys and girls can be expected to deepen throughout life. A lecture-presentation with discussion as the only method of teaching could not adequately convey the dynamic quality of a confession of faith. Other ways must be explored. "An Outline of the Faith" (p. 845ff, *BCP*) will be a useful content resource. The brief questions and answers are clear in their conciseness but assume more background knowledge than young candidates possess. The class noted earlier that was "a call to action" used a variety of methods suitable for younger learners. These included: games, films, small group experiences, prayer partners, poetry writing, banner and collage making, original crossword puzzles, trips away from the church, programs for parents, programs for the whole church, music, and role-playing. The conclusion: "Each class meeting was different, exciting and great fun."

The Confirmation service calls to attention what it means to follow Christ. The three questions of the baptismal covenant quoted earlier, are good starting-points. To proclaim by word and example is evangelism. How can a child share the faith with another person? It might be by inviting a new child at school or in the neighborhood to visit church. They can be offered occasions to visit other churches in order to understand the varieties of religious experience in their community. "To seek and serve Christ in all persons" is a powerful image to be translated into the lives of boys and girls. Explore with them ways that they can strive for justice and peace in school and family settings. The time set aside for the preparation for Confirmation needs to be sufficiently long so that those in the class can set themselves specific goals and begin to live in ways that will make a difference.

This is no invitation to now outdated Lenten practices when "don't" and "giving up" were the ways to prepare for Easter. This is a call to positive Christian discipleship where one can feel that God is helping a person to live more generously, forgivingly, lovingly; not by suppressing the self but by becoming more aware of others. Open-ended stories and role-plays, if these avoid easy moralisms, can help boys and girls see both the joy and pain of decision-making.

At this point consider the meaning of the Summary of the Law. Look at the Ten Commandments, and compare these with the Sermon on the Mount. The latter, as the introduction suggests, is a teaching for disciples, a law that can be kept only through grace. Boys and girls at this age can understand the meaning of law and grace as they could not earlier. Studies in child development indicate that younger children believe the punishment should fit the offense, with no "grace" given for intentionality. The illustration given from the studies of the Swiss pyschologist Jean Piaget is that of the child who broke twelve cups while reaching up to a shelf because mother had asked for help, and the child who broke two cups while reaching up to obtain something forbidden. Younger children would punish most the one who broke twelve cups. The intention to be helpful is not, to them, a mitigating (grace) factor.

Anyone who is about to assume the promises of Confirmation needs to be old enough to understand grace, for such a person surely stands in need of God's help in accepting forgiveness for the human failure to fulfill the promises made.

The Confirmation service does not leave people with promises made. They are "sealed in the Spirit" and this is symbolized by the chrism and the laying on of hands. For the boys and girls this will seem to be the climax of the service, and the personal meaning will be deepened by thoughtful consideration in advance. Consider carefully the prayer with the congregation, and that for each candidate (BCP, p. 418). Of all the notes sounded in the understanding of Confirmation, this is the most pervasive. Christians are called by the Holy Spirit. They respond because the Spirit enables them to do so. God the Holy Spirit empowers each person with gifts to live out the calling to follow Christ. You will want to explore with boys and girls the biblical meaning of the term, the way in which the Holy Spirit was made known in the early Christian community, and what is meant by the terms comforter, sustainer, enabler. Remember that the liturgical color for the event is red, signifying the tongues of flame and calling to remembrance the day of Pentecost. The words "inspiration" and "inspire" come from the word "spirit" and suggest breath, life. Paul addressed his letters to the "saints" at Corinth, Ephesus, meaning those who had been made holy because they were empowered by the Holy Spirit.

Confirmation and Church Membership

The preparation for Confirmation concludes with consideration of the fact that one is part of the Christian community. Those who witness the vows are asked to affirm that they will support these persons in their life in Christ (BCP, p. 303, 416). Who, then, is the church? This question will take you back to beginnings in the New Testament. You may want to allot one block of time to considering the nature of Christian worship. This should not be to repeat earlier preparation for the Eucharist but to concentrate on the meaning of worship: why Christians gather to engage in corporate praise and prayer.

One of the essential elements in any serious preparation for Confirmation is adequate time for those in the class really to form the habit of church attendance. You will want to observe what factors may be inhibiting: needing someone with whom to attend, restlessness, inability to understand and concentrate on the liturgy, lack of emotional response to hymn, Scripture, prayer, or Eucharist. This is not to suggest that worship should be a subjective experience into which people enter in order to "feel good." The way to avoid that approach is for people to learn why they do or do not "feel good" and how they can form a habit of participation as a fulfillment of their commitment and not because of what going to church on Sunday morning will do for them.

A simple form could be devised for class members either to think about or write simple answers each Sunday afternoon. What was the theme of the opening hymn? What feeling did it convey? What was the main idea in the Scripture lessons? Which among the prayers was closest to situations for which you usually pray? What one or two points can you remember from the sermon? If this kind of resume would be a burden instead of a help, simply make a point of talking about the service at the opening of each class session, encouraging boys and girls to bring you questions about what they did not understand or where they felt uncomfortable. If they understand the service sufficiently to feel involved, they can more likely be expected to continue the habit of attending after Confirmation. You will also want to remind sponsors, parents, teachers, and others in the parish that their part in affirming the confirmands is to assist young people by an invitation to sit with them or showing a welcome in other ways.

You will want to explore ways of helping boys and girls understand the new dimension of Christian life they are assuming because it is important for each to have an opportunity to grow. Some teachers have welcomed the learning center approach in which each person has a folder that lists the goal of the course, the contract (what each will learn and do) and specific tasks. Times together provide opportunities for presentations and to share learning. There are also times for working on tasks individually with Bibles, reference works, prayer books, tape recorders (both for presentations and for recording answers), and visual aids. The leader becomes a resource person and may have more individual contact with boys and girls than when the group is taught as a whole. The individual's folder would include a page for recording church attendance, perhaps with comments, and another page would list participation in other aspects of the life of the church. A page headed "Questions" encourages each to jot down perplexities to bring to either the priest or the class. The folder could include a devotional guide and/or brief daily Scripture readings. Because you want these girls and boys to become more aware of being part of the church, you could include a page of lined paper on which to list the names of people they know in the parish, encouraging them to add to this list week by week.

Clearly this is not an outline for a six-week course. The principal reason for the design is that the preparation for Confirmation is not simply a matter of learning material, although that may be one of the tasks. It is a time for cultivating the Christian life (the word "cultivate" is used advisedly) in girls and boys so that when the time of preparation is completed they will have a firm start toward participating regularly in worship, finding deepening meaning in prayer, feeling acquainted with other members of the parish, being comfortable as participants in the work and outreach of the parish—as ways of beginning to fulfill the promises they are assuming.

One way that other members support the newly confirmed is by receiving them as participants. You will want to explore how this can be done for boys and girls twelve years or younger. Notice them as persons: greet them, include them in conversation and expect them to be present. Another way is in the provision made for them. Are their classrooms equal in attractiveness and resourcess to those they know at school during the week? Do their teachers take the task seriously enough to be fully prepared each Sunday and ready to welcome questions and encourage inquiry? It has long been a tradition in Episcopal parishes for girls and boys to assume that Confirmation class was an exit from further religious education. With such a tradition, how can they understand what it means to be a Christian during the decision-making period called adolescence? How can such a parish develop the strong adult educational program needed to help people grow in their understanding? Sunday school teachers will need to be in close touch with the Confirmation class and its leader before, during, and after the sessions if a transition is to be made effectively, and the educational work begun in that class needs to be continued in some form through other channels. Few parishes have looked at this possibility with any creative seriousness.

The whole parish needs to find places where boys and girls can fulfill roles in its ministry and mission. The trend to intergenerational events can be a clue. Children can help with church meals and bazaars. They can be included with adult members singing Christmas carols in the community, making gifts for homes and hospitals. They can learn about the work of the church overseas and make their own contribution. The children's Lenten offering has been designed with this in mind but there are other opportunities. Some churches have children's choirs which provide direct service to the life of the parish. Special ways are needed through which the newly confirmed, during the year following, can become aware that they are needed and included in the work of the parish. This is the way to nurture in them a desire to serve and a sense of belonging.

All other members of the church are models to the young, and especially those adults with whom the girls and boys are most immediately in contact. From these older members the meaning of being a Christian is observed and learned.

Being Confirmed

Confirmation means affirming one's baptism, renewing commitment to Jesus as Lord, and sharing deeply in the Christian community. For those who are concerned that Confirmation has too often been a revolving door through which young members have come briefly into the life of the church and then exited, there may be help from others with the same concern. A yearbook on education from the Lutheran Church in America suggests that the age of Confirmation is not as important as the kind of preparation given. Essentially the tasks of this ministry of Confirmation are to help young people with the question of their identity as Christians, both individually and corporately; provide joint responsibilities and opportunities to work with adults; encourage adults to share and reveal themselves as they also are growing in Christ and in the life of the church.[8] The pastor alone cannot help young people fulfill their promises. Adult members need to have a serious commitment to being a nurturing congregation. One study has indicated that the activity level of parents will be reflected in the activity of the newly confirmed.[9] Not all confirmed children have parents who are active in the church so ways must still be found to assist these boys and girls become active in the worship and other ministries of the church.

In the fourth century, at a time when many people were becoming Christian, a series of catechetical lectures was written by Bishop Cyril in Jerusalem to prepare people for baptism. Attached to this is a briefer series, call the "Mystagogic Lectures."[10] These were spoken to the newly baptized during the week following the event, explaining the actions of Baptism; going into the water, receiving the white garment, lighting the candle, being anointed with oil. This experience indicated psychological and educational insight. It is one thing to have symbols explained in advance, and another to participate in an event. The impact raises new reflective questions.

The newly confirmed today also have questions after the event that they would not have had in preparation, and need clarifications they would not have thought about at the beginning. Before the event it is possible to explain the words. Only after the event can one explain the action. Promises take on a new solemnity after they have been made aloud before the bishop in the presence of the congregation. Confirmands can remember the feeling of being signed with oil, and receiving the laying on of hands. Actions have power. The preparation for Confirmation is not completed until whoever was responsible and who presented the confirmands provides sufficient opportunity for them to explore their feelings and responses. They need to share with one another what it means to be strengthened, empowered and sustained.

This is a "sending forth" of a group of boys and girls who, together with their priest, have explored meanings for a long time. Now they will cease to act as a group and assume individual commitments as members of the whole congregation.

These suggestions are intended to encourage fresh ways of looking at the preparation for confirmation with children. The goal is not to give information but to help girls and boys understand for themselves, and begin to implement in their own lives, the meanings of the promises each takes in the service of Christ within the life of the church. This kind of preparation requires careful planning and skilful use of methods and resources. Effectively accomplished, it is a step toward the growth and nurture of adolescents in the life of the church and will enrich the participation of children who now make their confession of faith.

Aspects of Adult Confirmation

John H. Westerhoff III

A clearer picture of our liturgical and catechetical future is beginning to emerge. On the once volatile issue of Christian initiation, the positions of those whose roots are planted in the Counter-Reformation are beginning to merge with those whose roots are set in the radical Reformation. We Episcopalians, who have always pictured ourselves as the bridge between these two poles, find ourselves caught in the pinch. Perhaps a few words describing what I have heard responsible and representative Anabaptist and Roman Catholic theologians saying will help to explain this rather bold contention.

Roman Catholics are advocating the Christian initiation of adults as theologically normative. Further, they are defending, as normative, a rite of adult initiation which unites Baptism, Confirmation and Eucharist into a single rite. The bishops, having already delegated the laying on of hands to their priests, are seriously discussing this single rite of initiation for infants as well as adults. Some theologians are arguing for the elimination of a separate sacrament of Confirmation for children and for a simple reception of Christians from other communions who unite with the Roman church.

Anabaptists who have always advocated a single initiation rite for adult believers have begun to argue that their present practice of baptizing children and adolescents has become a form of pseudobaptism to be seriously questioned. A few, however, have begun to discuss the wisdom of initiating children into the Christian faith by suggesting that the faith of the parents and of the church make an exception to the norm reasonable.

This leaves us Episcopalians somewhat caught in the middle, but as always hedging. Opinions about Christian initiation and Confirmation in the Episcopal Church remain confused and multiple. Differences abound: about what Confirmation means, about who is to administer it, about when it should occur, about whom it is for, and about what preparation is desirable.

The issue of Confirmation is different, of course, in every denomination. I have chosen, therefore, to write this essay from the perspective of the Episcopal church, my own tradition. Many of the insights and recommendations, however, will be relevant and useful to others.

To begin, some of us in the Episcopal Church argue for the theologically normative nature of an adult rite of initiation. Indeed, in the 1979 *Book of Occasional Services* there is a rite for the "Preparation of Adults for Holy Baptism" with directions for the proper catechesis of catechumens; it is modeled after the new Roman Catholic Rite of Adult Initiation (RCIA). In the 1979 *Book of Common Prayer* there is a new rite of "Thanksgiving for the Birth or Adoption of a Child," also. The presence of this rite raises some questions about the "necessity" of child Baptism; indeed, it suggests that infant Baptism should at least be delayed until a proper and adequate catechesis of parents and godparents can be accomplished.

Perhaps more significant is the renewed emphasis on Baptism found in the Prayer Book. The rubrics now call for a normative single rite of initiation—Baptism, Confirmation and Eucharist—to be celebrated when the bishop is present and a twofold rite—Baptism and Eucharist—to be celebrated by the priest as representative of the bishop at four other appropriate occasions: The Easter Vigil, the day of Pentecost, All Saint's day or the Sunday after and the Feast of the Baptism of our Lord (the First Sunday after Epiphany), all of which, interestingly, emphasize the gift of the Holy Spirit at Baptism. Futher, a new rite for "Reception into the Episcopal Church" for those who have already, in another tradition, been "confirmed" by the laying on of hands, has been added. This inclusion further encourages a new possible understanding for Confirmation.

More importantly, the 1979 *Book of Common Prayer* calls for the renewal of our baptismal covenant at least four times each year throughout our spiritual pilgrimage, from initiation to death. Thereby, Confirmation understood as the single reaffirmation of baptismal vows is contradicted. Further, a new repeatable rite for "Commitment to Christian Service" depreciates the understanding of Confirmation as a once and for all act of commitment to ministry. Thus, the Prayer Book now opens the way for the future, but some confines still remain and must be acknowledged.

In 1971 the House of Bishops stated explicitly that "Confirmation should not be regarded as a procedure of admission to the Holy Communion." As of that date, Baptism became the sole requirement for participation in the Eucharist. For many years we taught that Confirmation had to preceed First Communion. Once that change was made the issue of Confirmation surfaced again. In "An Outline of the Faith" in the 1979

Book of Common Prayer we read that Confirmation is a sacramental rite of the church in "which we express a mature commitment to Christ and receive strength from the Holy Spirit through prayer and the laying on of hands by a bishop." This statement in the Catechism leaves open a number of issues, the most important being a definition of "mature." To the Catechism's question: "What is required of those to be confirmed?" we read: "It is required of those to be confirmed that they have been baptized, are sufficiently instructed in the Christian faith, are penitent for their sins, and are ready to affirm their confession of Jesus Christ as Lord and Savior." While this helps a bit to define the who of Confirmation, the issue is still cloudy. What does it mean to be sufficiently instructed? When is one developmentally ready to repent of sins? My conviction is this: the criteria of "maturity," "sufficiently instructed," and readiness for confession minimally point to early adulthood. Of course, this discussion becomes somewhat academic considering both the inherited, unquestionable traditions in most parishes and the fact that the Canons of the church still read: "It shall be the duty of Ministers to prepare *young people* (italics mine) and others for Confirmation" (III:21–c).

Our existential situation is complicated further by our historic Episcopal twofold understanding of Confirmation. We choose not to make a choice between the medieval understanding which emphasizes the sevenfold gifts of the spirit at Confirmation establishing it a sacrament leading to maturity, a nurturing sacrament confirming the grace of a strengthening power to aid persons in their pilgrimage to full humanity, and the Renaissance-Reformation understanding which emphasizes a personal, mature assumption of the vows made for a person by their sponsors and the church at their Baptism, a sacrament celebrating arrival at mature, owned faith and confirming the grace of strengthening power to live out this commitment.

The prayers for Confirmation in the 1979 *Book of Common Prayer* embody these two alternatives. The second, appropriate for child or adolescent Confirmation (similar to the Roman Catholic sacrament of Confirmation which emphasizes the sevenfold gifts of the Spirit) dates from the 1552 *Prayer Book*, but contains one significant revision: "Child" is replaced by "servant," underlying a growing conviction that Confirmation is not necessarily an act appropriate for children. It reads: "Defend, O Lord, your servant N. with your heavenly grace, that *he* may continue yours forever and daily increase in your Holy Spirit more and more until *he* comes to your everlasting kingdom. *Amen.*"

The first prayer (and as such, I suggest, the preferred) drafted by the late Urban T. Holmes is more appropriate to adult Confirmation. It reads: "Strengthen, O Lord, your servant N. with your Holy Spirit, empower *him* for service and sustain *him* all the days of his life. *Amen*"; it is a prayer which has a character similar to the consecration prayer for deacons and priests; likewise its major thrust is empowerment "for God's service" or ministry.

While wisely continuing to leave open a variety of understandings and ways, the 1979 *Book of Common Prayer* does point to a future in which, as far as Confirmation remains a separate sacramental rite, it is to be normatively understood as an adult rite.

In the rubrics prior to the Confirmation rite we read: "In the course of their Christian development, those baptized at an early age are expected, when they are ready and have been duly prepared *to make a mature public affirmation of their faith and commitment to the responsibilities of their Baptism* (italics mine) and to receive the laying on of hands by the bishop."

Immediately following we read: "Those baptized as adults, unless baptized with the laying on of hands by a Bishop are also expected to (do as above)." The implicit connection between Confirmation and adult initiation is obvious; thus, once again, indicating a preference for adult Confirmation.

There are, of course, practical as well as theological and liturgical reasons to defend adult Confirmation. Almost a decade ago, while still a minister in the United Church of Christ and editor of *Colloquy*, an ecumenical magazine on education in church and society, I edited an issue on Confirmation (May-June, 1974) which questioned Confirmation as a rite appropriate or relevant to adolescence. I further questioned Confirmation as either theologically or culturally adequate for an adolescent rite of passage. I also questioned whether Confirmation should be understood as a rite establishing church membership, whether people should be encouraged to make a commitment to the church early in adolescence, and whether or not Confirmation of adolescents was appropriate to a mature understanding of Christian faith and life. In that same issue I advocated an understanding of infant Baptism which established persons as full members of the Christian community and entitled them to Holy Communion, a continuous lifelong renewal of baptismal vows, and a minimal age of eighteen (twelfth grade) for Confirmation, understood as a mature faith commitment to ministry in the world.

Within the next three years I published two other articles on Confirmation. The first was entitled "Joining the Church or Witnessing to Faith: Initiation Rites in Protestant Churches" (*Character Potential: A Record f Research*, Spring-Summer, 1978). In this research essay I revealed my dings that Confirmation was functionally understood in most mainline Protestant churches as a rite of church membership, a rite which proved to have negative results; namely, it acted as a graduation exercise that put an end to spiritual growth, a continuing quest for a reasonable faith, and even to participation in the life of the church. Instead of encouraging faith commitment and ministry I found that more than 50 percent of those confirmed during adolescence dropped out of active church membership shortly thereafter. In *Liturgy* (September, 1977) I published an essay entitled "Betwixt and Between" which questioned adolescent Confirmation as an appropriate act of faith commitment and suggested the need for a more appropriate rite of identity. I suggested a covenant of discipleship rite which, as one step in their lifelong pilgrimage to live into their Baptism, would celebrate this significant turning point in their lives, and prepare, affirm and empower them for the next step in their spiritual journey by having them publicly take responsibility for their faith and life as baptized Christians already members of the community of Christian faith.

Since then I have explored this subject in a number of books. While my position has been continually maturing and to some extent, therefore, changing, it has maintained a high degree of consistency and indeed correspondence to Episcopal Church theology and practice. To catch a glimpse of my ever evolving thought I suggest the reader review the following: Chapter 8, "Identity and the Pilgrimage of Faith" in Gwen Kennedy Neville and Westerhoff, *Learning Through Liturgy*, Seabury, 1978; Chapter 4, "Personal Growth in Identity" in Westerhoff and William Willimon, *Liturgy and Learning Through the Life Cycle*, Seabury, 1980; and Chapter 10, "Framing an Alternative Future for Catechesis" in Westerhoff and O.C. Edwards (eds.), *A Faithful Church: Issues in the History of Catechesis*, Morehouse-Barlow, 1981.

Ideally, permit me to paint a picture of my vision for the future. First, I envision a single rite of initiation combining Baptism, Confirmation and Eucharist, administered by a bishop or a priest as the bishop's representative. I believe that from a theologically normative perspective this should be an adult rite, with the reasonable and indeed recommended exception for the children of the faithful, legitimated by the faith of the church and its representatives, the child's sponsors; i.e., godparents. In either case, Baptism is to be understood as the beginning of a spiritual pilgrimage, a journey of living into one's Baptism, of sanctification or the process of becoming who we already are; that is, the justified and redeemed person acknowledged at our Baptism. I affirm the renewal of our baptismal covenant at least five times each year throughout our faith journey: namely, the visitation of the bishop, the Easter Vigil, All Saints Day, Pentecost and the Baptism of our Lord. I contend that before each of these celebrations an opportunity for congregational catechetical preparation should be encouraged. Further, the opportunity for special personal preparation and renewal should be provided. While such special efforts might occur at any point in a person's lifetime, particular times seem appropriate. For example, at age six, when preparation might take the form of reflective activities related to the person's experience of having been a participant in the Holy Communion; at age ten or eleven, when a person might be helped to understand life in the community of faith and the meaning of Christian service; at age sixteen, when a person might be prepared to assume responsibility for faith and life and be provided with the skills most necessary for the continuing journey—for example, skills in biblical interpretation and theological and moral reflection; and sometime in the late twenties or after, when a person might be prepared to make a mature faith commitment, discern the place of ministry to which God is now calling, and be prepared for that ministry. There will of course be numerous other times in the adult pilgrimage that a special renewal might be celebrated. However, whenever these moments occur the church will need to provide a catechetical experience to prepare persons for this unique next step in their lives and will need to celebrate this personal renewal in a special manner at the same time as the congregation, in general, renews its baptismal covenant.

It might look like this: On the five occasions when baptisms are celebrated some would, whatever their age, participate in this threefold rite of initiation for the first time; some would come forward to make a special renewal of their baptismal covenant (and perhaps have hands laid upon them); and the rest of the congregation would make a general renewal of their vows. All would have been appropriately prepared. In this way catechesis appropriate to the stage in one's journey could be provided, an opportunity for marking important spiritual transitions in our spiritual journey celebrated, and the whole community reminded of their continuing need to grow into their Baptism.

Now that is ideal and while desired I suspect a way off. What do we do in the meantime? While I can support an adolescent rite of Confirmation understood as celebrating a person's taking responsibility for faith and life, of promising to continue the quest for a reasonable faith and a moral commitment to ministry in church and society and of imparting the gifts of the Spirit to aid in this continuing pilgrimage, I am concerned that if we perpetuate this rite the church will still be without a significant way to celebrate, let alone prepare people for, a mature faith commitment to Christian service.

As long as we continue to perpetuate a separate sacramental rite of Confirmation administered by the bishop, I want to argue strongly for celebrating Confirmation in adulthood and I want to advocate an understanding of the Confirmation rite that perceives it as calling forth the Holy Spirit to "ordain" adults for their ministry in church and society. I defend this position on fundamentally practical theological grounds: namely, that the future of a faithful church is dependent upon the lives of spiritually mature, theologically knowledgeable, morally committed adults. By maintaining the theological norm of both adult Baptism and adult Confirmation we witness to that conviction and provide the means for its actualization.

Having made, I trust, my argument for adult Confirmation, let me turn to the catechetical dimension of this sacramental rite. To begin, let me suggest that no matter how we understand the rite or when we celebrate it the key to its meaning and relevance will be found in the catechesis we provide. Unless we put our major attention on this dimension of the rite our liturgical discussions will matter little.

Infants, children and adolescents, no less than adult Christians, need an opportunity on numerous occasions to reflect on their lives and faith and to affirm their commitment to Christ and his service in a variety of ways throughout their lives in the Christian faith community. Christian commitment cannot be seen as a single act, but rather one that once made needs to be continually renewed.

The church has agreed that the sacrament of Baptism is a rite of incorporation into Christ and entry into membership in Christ's church. It is a single non-repeatable rite of initiation, whatever the age at which it is administered, which grants admission to the sacrament of the Eucharist and which requires no further ritual to make it complete. However, we recognize that Baptism is only the initial step in an ongoing process of Christian maturity. The Baptism of people at varying stages of maturation reflects both divine gift and human appropriation, corporate and individual response, childlike trust and mature responsibility.

Nevertheless, in so far as we interpret Confirmation primarily as a rite in which we renew our baptismal vows and equip persons for a mature apostolate, we need to take Christian formation with greater seriousness and provide adults with a catechetical and liturgical opportunity for a mature, individual profession of faith and personal commitment to the life and mission of the church.

We have advocated adult Confirmation. It is important, therefore, to explain how we are using the word. Typically we use "adult" to mean a particular chronological age, but there is no way to determine and no agreement on the year that distinguishes an adult from a child. In any case, by adult Confirmation we do not mean Confirmation of those who are no longer children. If we had intended that meaning we would have referred to the Confirmation of adults.

In this essay we are using the word adult to refer to a pyschosocial ideal, an ideal which should guide persons in their decision to seek

Confirmation. An adult from our perspective has reached a place in life in which three capacities and inclinations have begun consciously to emerge. While one lives into these throughout the rest of one's adult life, a transition period marks an appropriate time for Confirmation.

While childhood is dominated by nonrational, dependent and non-productive capacities and inclinations, adolescence is dominated by rational, independent and productive ones. Adulthood as we are using the word points to the stage in life when an integration of these polar opposites begins: first, when a person is able to move from life experience to the nonrational (i.e., imagination) to the rational; that is, can use reason in the service of visionary life; secondly, when a person is able to live an interdependent life of mutuality; that is, of reciprocally giving and receiving; and thirdly, when a person is able to give life in the service of another, to care for and love others unconditionally; that is, to be productive by self-giving, a nonproductive act.

Confirmation, therefore, is appropriate for three groups of adults: (1) those who have been baptized but never received the sacrament of Confirmation, (2) those persons from other Christian bodies preparing to be received into the Episcopal Church, and (3) those who have been baptized and confirmed as Episcopalians, but would like to make a personal public reaffirmation of their baptismal vows. It is my contention that the catechetical aims for all these should be the same, though the particular catechesis should be adopted to meet the special needs of each person. In that same regard I recommend that no particular amount of time or program be established for everyone. After inquiry classes, whose aim is to establish readiness, and a personal interview with the priest to establish commitment, the confirmand and the priest should identify a sponsor who will accompany the confirmand through the time of preparation. At the same time an appropriate process for preparation can be designed.

In any case, it would be a serious mistake to use Confirmation catechesis as an introduction to Episcopal history, polity and practice. Confirmation should not be understood as a means of creating Episcopalians. It is assumed that persons, prior to Confirmation catechesis in an Episcopal church, will be familiar, through active participation in an Episcopal church, with the understandings and ways of the Episcopal church and that any questions or concerns pertaining to the Episcopal Church would have been addressed during the inquiry sessions prior to preparation for Confirmation.

Lutheran and Calvinist churches are doctrinal; for them doctrine is primal. For Episcopalians *The Book of Common Prayer* is normative for belief; traditionally we have moved from liturgy to theology to action. Our movement is from symbolic actions to reflection, to daily life, to reflection, and back again to symbolic actions. Thus it is appropriate that we look at the rite of Baptism for insight as to the proper catechesis for the renewal of that covenant in the rite of Confirmation.

We Episcopalians have a sincere commitment to a "reasonable faith." We need continually to affirm that disciplined passion for reason of which Richard Hooker spoke in identifying the source of authority in Anglicanism. Correspondingly, one aim of Christian formation is the ability to think theologically and morally, that is, to think rightly about religious experience and action. That is what we mean by orthodoxy, a cognitive process of "right judgment." We can accept neither a pietistic anti-intellectualism nor a dogmatic sterile intellectualism. It is the unity of head and heart, cognition and affect by a complementary process of growth into wholeness that we advocate. As Urban T. Holmes put it in his 1979 Robinson T. Orr Lectures at Huron College, Ontario, Canada, "We have a commitment to a reasonable belief which leads us to the experience of God's love and tests our claims to the outcome of that experience."

The process of spiritual growth, to mature in faith, is the development of a conscience and consciousness. While the inclination to confess Jesus as Lord and Savior is laudatory, it is evidence of a change in one's relationship to self and others as a result of coming to know God in Christ which we desire. It is not what people say they feel that makes the difference in human life, but rather the actions which result from the in-tegration of feeling and thinking, intuition and intellect, imagination and reason. To quote Holmes again, "The outcome of the experience of God in Christ should be a heightened consciousness which becomes the basis for action which is virtuous."

Aristotle explained that there are three ways of knowing: *theoria*, *poiesis* and *praxis*. *Theoria* is an objective, disinterested reflection upon the world and is concerned with knowledge for its own sake—it is predominantly reflection. *Praxis* is the integration of *theoria* and *poiesis*, combining action and reflection; it is action that is reflectively done, or reflection in action. Aristotle equated *praxis* with living the ethical life. As such, it is particularly appropriate to Confirmation catechesis whose aim is apostolic life. *Praxis* is also appropriate to the relationship between liturgy and catechesis. As we have said, we move from liturgical action, to reflection, to apostolic action, to reflection, and back to liturgical action. Catechesis for Confirmation must employ *praxis* as its way of knowing. Confirmation catechesis, therefore, begins by requiring us to examine our individual lives in terms of our thinking, feeling and doing. Secondly, it requires us to reflect on the meanings contained in our baptismal covenant. Thirdly, it requires us to ask what the symbolic words and actions of this liturgy say to our life, and what our lives say to the liturgy. And lastly, it requires us to discern what action God is calling us to so that we might give ourselves to those actions during the renewal of our baptismal covenant.

Dame Julian of Norwich, one of the great fourteenth century English lay mystics, wrote, "Man (sic) endures in this life by three things, by which three God is honored and we are furthered, protected and saved. The first is the use of natural reason. The second is the common teachings of Holy Church. The third is the inward grace giving operation of the Holy Spirit; and these three are all from one God." Her classical Anglican viewpoint is amazingly contemporary and constitutes a *praxial* catechesis for adult Confirmation.

We need to grow our awareness of the process by which we make sense of ourselves in our world. This process during the adult period of our lives is an exploration of experience within the life of the Christian community illumined by our corporate memory and enlightened by use of reason.

Ministry belongs to the church as a whole—when we were baptized we were baptized into a ministry. Serious theological reflection is essential to effective ministry. Preparation for adult Confirmation is best understood, therefore, as the process by which we make a concentrated effort to aid persons to discern the particular ministry to which God is calling them at this moment in their pilgrimage and to equip them for an effective ministry as believers in Jesus Christ and members of his church.

Our catechetical aims, therefore, are best derived from the liturgy. The primary intention of the liturgy is encompassed in two prayers. The first is prayed by the bishop after the confirmands renew their baptismal covenant. It begs God to be party to this renewal of promises once made by the community for the person, or by the person in another context. It further asks God to send them forth in the power of the Holy Spirit to perform the service God has set before them.

The second prayer is prayed following the laying on of hands by the bishop. It asks God through the Holy Spirit to be with them, leading them in the knowledge and obedience of his Word that they may serve God in this life and dwell with God in the life to come. Thus, the thrust of Confirmation is conveyed as sanctification, that is, sustaining us in our relationship to God and empowering us for service to our neighbor. It is the same apostolic thrust that encompasses the eucharistic liturgy which closes when the deacon (the symbol bearer of service) exclaims, "Let us go forth to love and serve the Lord" and the congregation cries out, "Thanks be to God," as they exit in song to commence their liturgy of ministry in the world. It is for mission and ministry that the sacraments of the church grant us grace. Thus, our catechetical aims must focus upon and emphasize this apostolic understanding of the sacramental rite of Confirmation.

In order to surface the particular apostolic understanding in the Confirmation rite we need to explore it in detail: The sponsors having presented the confirmands they have helped to prepare, the bishop asks: "*Do you reaffirm your renunciation of evil?*" It is important to recall that at Baptism a person turns away from and therefore negates the power of three kinds of evil—cosmic evil, or those spiritual forces that rebel against God, for example, natural tragedies; social evil, or those institutions and systems we humans create that disrupt and destroy persons, for example, war, systemic racism and sexism; and personal evil, or those sinful desires which draw us from the love of God, for example, greed, lust, pride and avarice.

Do you renew your commitment to Jesus Christ? In the baptismal liturgy we announce our turning away from evil and our turning to Jesus Christ, who saves us from the evil one and thereby makes it possible for us to be whole and holy. We further announce that we are putting our trust in his grace or unmerited love as the means by which we can actualize our new life. And lastly, we promise to follow and obey him, that is to live a life that is a sign and witness to that gift.

Catechetically, we need to help persons reflect on their lives, to examine who or what has power over their lives and to whom or what they are giving their loyalty and to explore the perceptions which inform their lives by reviewing our understanding of the Christian story—our corporate memory of how God has been active in the history of the world and of our people in the past and present; also by considering our understanding of the Christian vision—our picture of the reign of God, where in human history justice, peace, equity, freedom, unity and well-being prevail; that is, where love triumphs over hate, hope over despair and life over death. After we have renewed our faith through a rational examination of our story and vision we can continue.

Apostles' Creed. The next element in the renewal of our baptismal covenant is a reaffirmation of the Apostles' Creed or those convictions about God as Creator, Redeemer and Sanctifier to which we give our hearts and loyalty. In this context the catechetical aim is intellectually to explore the meanings behind this love song and its implications for individual and corporate life.

For some, the books *Christian Believing* and *Understanding the Faith of the Church* in *The Church's Teaching Series* might be helpful. In any case, it is important to work toward an understanding of each part of the trinitarian formula expressed in the Creed and its implications. For example, we need to reflect on what it means to say that God is Creator and that we are made in the image of God. I suggest that at least normatively it implies an affirmation of procreation and preservation of all life, no matter how deformed. And, if we can affirm such a view, what does it imply for our lives? Secondly, what does it mean to say that God is our Redeemer? I suggest that, since Christ dies for all, it implies that every life is of ultimate value, even the least among us. Since this affirmation calls us to do likewise we need, for example, to examine where racism, sexism, classism, nationalism, denominationalism, are present in our individual or corporate lives. Thirdly, we need to reflect on what it means to say God is our Sanctifier, the one who makes life whole and holy. I suggest that minimally it affirms the essential nature of community and deplores anything that divides or distorts individuals or communities.

Having reflected on the Creed, its meanings and implications, we are ready to turn to the specific promises related to the living out of the baptismal covenant as expressed in the Apostles' Creed. I suggest that at each step the confirmand be encouraged to explore past and present actions and to move toward some specific commitments in terms of each promise.

The questions follow: "*Will you continue in the apostles' teaching and fellowship, in the breaking of bread and in the prayers?*" Behind this promise is a commitment to a rational study of the holy Scriptures, to life in an historic faith community, to participation in the eucharistic liturgies of the church, and to the fulfillment of the spiritual life. Serious attention to both biblical interpretation and meditation on the Scriptures may need to be given. For some, *The Bible For Today's Church* may be helpful. To participate in the fellowship of an historic community is to have a sense of one's history. *The Church in History* is particularly helpful, since it places our Anglican tradition in historical context. Participation in the Eucharist provides another opportunity to reflect on the meaning of the Eucharist and the liturgical life of the church. For some *Liturgy for Living* will be a useful resource. And last, the promise to live the spiritual life encourages us to develop a spiritual discipline. *Living In the Spirit* can be an excellent resource.

"*Will you persevere in resisting evil and whenever you fall into sin, repent and return to the Lord?*" Here is an opportunity to learn about and participate in the rite of reconciliation. But it is also a time to reflect on how we might best resist both social and personal evil and to engage in whatever form of catechesis seems best to encourage, sustain and support such behavior. It is a time to reflect on the seven deadly sins and the practice of the virtues. What is most important, however, is that the confirmand develop a program for the practice of the virtues.

"Will you proclaim by word and example the Good News of God in Christ?" Here is an opportunity to reflect on those for whom the good news is announced: the hurt, the captive, the oppressed, the sick, the hungry, the needy, the lost, the troubled, all those denied the benefits of life in God's redeemed world. It is a time to reflect on "acts evangelism," or the means by which we bring through action good news to those who only know the bad news of the evening report and then when asked why we do so to be able to tell the story of Jesus. It means our asking how we can be a sign of God's reign in the lives of all people and make an evangelical witness to God's kingdom come. It is also a time for us to reflect on the Good News as it speaks to our lives and to share our experience of the redeeming love of God.

"Will you seek to serve Christ in all persons, loving your neighbor as yourself?" Here is an opportunity to reflect on the meaning of ministry in church and society, to strive to discern the ministry to which God is calling us at this point in our lives, that is, to help the confirmands to discern to what voluntary service in the community or church or particular occupation they are being called, and to prepare them for engaging in this ministry. The book *The Christian Moral Vision* may provide a resource for some.

And last: *"Will you strive for justice and peace among all people and respect the dignity of every human being?"* Here is an opportunity to reflect on our personal and corporate social action. Most persons in the church can understand acts of Christian service to the needy but have difficulty understanding social, political, economic action that affects the social situation in ways that make our acts of mercy unnecessary. This is also a time to reflect on how we indirectly or directly support actions in our community, church, nation, state, or place of work which work for liberation and justice, reconciliation and peace. More importantly, it is a time to decide what we can do to change those social structures which prevent God's *shalom*.

All in all the catechesis which needs to be developed for each person depends on his or her knowledge, on where one is in the spiritual pilgrimage and on particular needs. Alone, with their sponsors or in small groups over whatever period of time is necessary, persons need to be prepared for this commitment to ministry.

We need to make sure that persons are truly ready to take this significant step and that they are committed to a serious preparation. This sacramental rite cannot be taken too seriously. Some may not be ready until they are thirty, forty, or even fifty years of age. Until that time they can be nurtured by sacramental life in the church and by a regular renewal of their baptismal covenant. Nevertheless, when the time is right a period of formation and instruction which makes use of human experience and life in the church to deepen their Christian understanding, commitment and action are essential. Such preparation is the responsibility of the bishop, who shares it with priests, deacons, sponsors and lay catechists. When this responsibility is once again assumed by the whole church, mutuality of ministry and a faithful church will begin to emerge, thereby providing God with an instrument of mission and ministry for the gospel.

The Parish Context for Confirmation Intentions

Kendig Brubaker Cully

Although Confirmation is a subject for extensive liturgical, historical and theological analysis, ultimately it has to do with the intentions of real persons in an actual community. One is never a Christian in lonely isolation, nor does the community of the church exist without the participation in it of the many individuals who have affirmed their intention, through Baptism and Confirmation, to be ingrafted into it. The point and place in which all the formal actions of the Christian community receive their origin, their continuation, and their validation is the congregation of the faithful. Translated into ecclesial usage, this means the parish church.[1]

Some bishops prefer to exercise their episcopal role in the setting of a cathedral, yet in the American church there are only a few instances of pure cathedrals in the sense of being the "bishop's church," without an enrolled constituency of members. Most cathedrals, in this country, have been parish churches elevated to cathedral status at some time after a diocese has become thoroughly established and reached the point at which the dignity of housing the *cathedral* has been perceived as a desideratum. Even after such churches have been elevated to cathedral status, they continue for the most part to function as parishes. From time to time the bishop may choose to bring candidates for Confirmation into the cathedral for the ceremonial function, rather than to lay hands on individuals in their home churches. But the cathedral itself usually will have its own "Confirmation class," and the dean will present its congregation's candidates in approximately the same manner as will the rector of a parish or the vicar of a mission in those bailiwicks.

Regardless of the status of a cathedral as the principal locale of operation for diocesan-wide events of worship and otherwise, it is the parish church that will continue to be the scene of those ecclesial events which most influence the ongoing life of the members of the church community. It is on annual visitations to a parish that the bishop will continue to confirm (and baptize, too, if the traditional role of the bishop in that regard is ever again taken seriously, though the delegation of that function to parish clergy, the prevalent norm, shows no sign of diminution). It is in the parish church that the new confirmands will show the degree of their commitment in terms of their attendance at worship and participation in other parish functions. It is therefore important to examine some of the implications of the parish context for the fulfillment of Confirmation intentionality.

In the first place, as we have suggested already, the parish church is where most of the members of the church meet the bishop and come to sense a relationship with him. Although the bishop may be acknowledged as president of the Eucharist, the one who baptizes (or, in both instances the one in whose name the local pastor exercises these functions), and the chief pastor who administers church affairs from an office in the see city, actually it is in Confirmation that the people really come to understand the bishop's role as their chief pastor. By individually receiving the laying-on-of-hands from the bishop the members sense their relationship to the larger, universal church. No one else can with the same authority remind them, as the Confirmation prayer puts it, that they are strengthened with the Holy Spirit, empowered for the Lord's service, and given sustenance all the days of their life. To be sure, such words might equally well be spoken by a priest, but when the Confirmation prayer is said by the bishop, it is received with the full force of the function as chief pastor.

The parish church is, furthermore, the locale of the total activity of those who constitute the Body of Christ in that particular situation. The parish obviously cannot be thought of any longer as a purely geographical concept—that is, embracing all the people who live in a given agreed area of a city, or in an entire county or town. This never was a part of the American church scene, at least after the demise of the earlier establishments (such as Anglicanism in Virginia or Congregationalism in several New England colonies). Even the most centrally organized hierarchical system—that of the Roman Catholic Church—had to give way, in the twentieth century, on that strict geographic designation of official parishes, as, indeed, it did on the related, but not completely identical, principle of ethnic assignment to parishes. Instead, a parish has become, in practically all the denominations, an assemblage of persons who for a multitude of reasons prefer to be associated with such-and-such a congregation. People have been known to travel vast distances in order to be present in their chosen parish churches, the reason for such fidelity ranging from preference for a particular theological or liturgical style, to the attractiveness of certain clergy, the sponsoring of certain programs or groups which are found to be congenial, or loyalty to a tradition of family involvement in a particular church.

In the Confirmation rite, after addressing to the candidates the questions concerning renunciation of evil and renewal of commitment to Jesus Christ, the bishop asks the congregation: "Will you who witness these vows do all in your power to support these persons in their life in Christ?" After their "We will" response, the entire congregation, bishop, confirmands and all those already confirmed previously, renew their own baptismal covenant by repeating the Apostles' Creed in the form of answers to a catechetical-type question. In other words, there is a mutuality of awareness on the part of all concerned that together they are called upon to be Christ's Body in that place and time, and in relation with one another in that congregationl setting.[2]

The implication of this liturgical action is that the members will seek to implement their baptismal and Confirmation experience in terms of the day-by-day life of their church. They will seek to sustain one another in times of need—expressing a pastoral concern for one another. They will gather strength from their mutual worship of God for being as Christ together in the world. They will remember that in his name they are called to be channels of his grace to all in the community with whom they come in contact, whether the neighbors be friendly or unfriendly, lovable or unlovable, rich or poor, black or white or yellow or red, male or female. This will mean that their own common life will contain both mutual spiritual edification and mutual Christian service. They have covenanted in Christ's name and Spirit to be a caring community, a loving, gracious, serving company of those whose minds and wills have been claimed for his own service.

If there were no such spiritual reality within a congregation, it is questionable as to whether Confirmation could really legitimately be offered in their midst. It is an action that assumes a supportive, encouraging, sustaining role on the part of the community in which the Confirmation vows are executed. The implications of this for the worshipping, serving, studying parish community are vast. The positive aspects are that a congregation will certainly desire to explore all the avenues through which such a community can be cultivated in a local situation. Negatively stated, a church needs to examine its life with ruthless honesty in order to find ways to eradicate from its corporate life any element that hinders it from being, indeed, Christ's Body in that place.[3]

The fulfillment of the congregation's pledge in the Confirmation rite will involve goals and activities in every aspect of the church's life. A parish needs to take with utmost seriousness every phase of its life in order to fulfill that pledge. In recent years the consciousness of this necessity has begun to penetrate the conscience and efforts of both denominational executives and local clergy of practically every American church body. It has been apparent in the Episcopal Church in programmatic emphases emanating from national church offices in New York and in the conferences and workshops sponsored in many places by agencies such as the College of Preachers and the Alban Institute in Washington, D.C., and the various theological seminaries, especially in relation to outreach services, seminars and lay study programs.

In-depth studies have been indicating that church life has too often been carried on at the level of external growth considerations. Evangelism often has been interpreted as adding new members, teaching as indoctrinating, and preaching as purely spiritualizing the gospel of Jesus Christ. The realization has been dawning on the churches that evangelism must spring from the very nature of our Christian commitment, teaching must deal not only with passing on cognitive data but with nurturing the whole person in total life situations through dynamic faith, and preaching must stir up as well as provide solace.[4]

The intentionality of the congregation, as represented in the promise to do all in their power to support the confirmands in their life of Christ, is, of course, related to the prior affirmation (a few seconds earlier in the rite itself) of the candidates that they reaffirm their renunciation of evil and their commitment to Jesus Christ. It should be obvious, but is not always so, that if one takes this seriously, it will be necessary for a Christian to seek every opportunity to fulfill those promises. The life of the congregation conceivably could be so arranged that every encouragement is given to the confirmed to live out those vows.

There must also be an intentionality on the part of the person being confirmed. One must seek to work for the eradication of the evils one has promised to deplore forever. One must constantly examine oneself to ascertain if commitment to Jesus Christ is really the operative *motif* of one's life. How does this commitment find expression in relations both with other members of the Christian community and with the world outside the church? Is one's moral stance actual as well as verbal? Is there evidence by one's stewardship of time, money and talents that one is honest in commitment to Jesus' way of life? Continual self-examination through prayer is indicated as a minimal requirement for the simplest keeping of such a promise. Thus we can say that the congregation is both the training-ground for personal piety and the channel through which the Judeo-Christian insistence upon God's justice and love can be projected into the total social order.[5]

Notes

Chapter 1. Confirmation in the Episcopal Church and in the Church of England (Fuller).

[1] In this paper the English Reformation is regarded as a process lasting from 1534 to 1662. The Prayer Book of 1662 will be regarded as the final form achieved by the Anglican Reformation.

[2] The form of "Baptism for those of Riper Years" was first introduced in 1662 for those who had not been baptized during the Commonwealth period. It was hoped that it would henceforth be useful for baptizing "natives in our plantation," i.e., American Indians. This service was merely an adaptation of the rite of infant Baptism. No adjustment of Confirmation (e.g., the integration of it with Baptism by the omission of the renewal of vows) was made, and no directive given for the admission of those baptized and confirmed in the Lutheran and Reformed traditions, let alone in English nonconformity, which hardly then existed.

[3] The 1662 rubric conceded the admission to Communion to those "ready and desirous to be confirmed." The clear intention here was that communicants should have made a public profession of faith. The Reformers did not regard Confirmation as an integral part of sacramental initiation.

[4] Speaking of "Confirmation" in Reformation Anglicanism, Marion J. Hatchett quite rightly observes that "The order of some components and portions of certain texts may resemble the rite called "confirmation" in the medieval books, but the rationale is clearly that of the Consultation [of Hermann of Cologne] and other German church orders." Marion J. Hatchett, *Commentary on the American Prayer Book*, The Seabury Press, 1981, p. 264.

[5] See Hatchett, *ibid.*, pp. 259–60. Despite Bucer's views, Confirmation by the local pastor became the normal practice even in those Lutheran churches which retained episcopacy.

[6] Jeremy Taylor, "*A Discourse of Confirmation,*" *Works*, vol. III, Bohn, 1853, pp. 3–31.

[7] The patristic school has included the following:

F.W. Puller, *What is Distinctive of Confirmation?*, 1980.
A.J. Mason, The Relation of Confirmation to Baptism, Longmans, Green, 1981.
Gregory Dix, *The Theology of Confirmation in Relation to Baptism*, Dacre, 1946.
Lionel S. Thornton, *Confirmation Today*, Dacre, 1946.
——, *Confirmation: Its Place in the Baptismal Mystery*, Dacre, 1953.
J.G. Davies, *The Spirit, the Church and the Sacraments*, Faith, 1954.
Cyril E. Pocknee, *The Rites of Christian Initiation*, Mowbray, 1962.
——, *Water and the Spirit*, Darton, Longman and Todd, 1967.
J.D.C. Fisher, *Christian Initiation: Baptism in the Medieval West*, SPCK, 1963.
——, *Christian Initiation: The Reformation Period*, SPCK, 1970.
——, *Confirmation and the Ely Report*, Church Literature Association, 1971.
——, "*Confirmation and Commitment,*" *The Anglican Catholic* (1973) 4–7.

———, "A Critique of Prayer Book Studies 26," *The Anglican Catholic* (1974) 2–6.

———, *Confirmation Then and Now*, Alcuin Club/SPCK, 1978.

Some of the above scholars advocated the "reintegration" of the BCP rites of Baptism and "Confirmation." Others, notably Dix, were content to preserve the traditional Anglican practice but to give it a "patristic" interpretation—a line which O.C. Quick, *The Christian Sacraments*, Nisbet, 1927, 184 castigated as "intolerable." Yet again, others were content to retain the full sacramental initiation of infants (often including First Communion) while others opted for exclusively adult initiation.

8 The medievalists include:

A.T. Wirgman, *The Doctrine of Confirmation*, 1897.

O.C. Quick, as above.

A.M. Ramsey, Reviewing Thronton's 1946 pamphlet, *Theology* 19 (1946), 248–49.

A.E.J. Rawlinson, *Christian Initiation*, SPCK, 1947.

G.W.F. Lampe, *The Seal of the Spirit*, Longmans, Green, 1951, may be included here, though he insists that throughout the patristic period water Baptism was full sacramental initiation and the accompanying ceremonies explicative of certain aspects thereof. The Confirmation rite of 1662 he interprets on Reformation rather than on medieval lines.

9 E.g., that the Holy Spirit was given in Baptism for adoption to sonship, and in Confirmation as a strengthening for Christian discipleship; that the Spirit works externally in Baptism, effecting regeneration, and internally in Confirmation, effecting the indwelling presence.

10 It is notable that all of the writers named in footnotes 7 and 8, with the exception of Lampe, were Anglo-Catholics. There was a deep division among them which has confounded the confusion and made it impossible to claim that there is a single "Catholic" view. Both groups agreed, however, that Confirmation was a sacrament conveying the Holy Spirit. Both groups resorted to strained interpretations of the 1662 text.

11 American 1892, Canadian 1917, English 1927–8, American 1928.

12 *Confirmation To-day: Interim Report of the Canterbury and York Joint Committees*, SPCK, 1944.

13 Frank Bennett, "Indiscriminate Confirmation," *Theology* 48 (1945) , 73–77.

A.M. Ramsey, "Doctrine of Confirmation," *Theology* 48 (1945), pp. 194–201.

C.F.D. Moule, "Baptism with Water and the Holy Ghost," *Theology* 48 (1945), pp. 246–49.

Sherwin Bailey, "Baptism and the Outpouring of the Holy Spirit in the New Testament," *Theology* 49 (1946), pp. 11–14.

R.H. Fuller, "Baptism and Confirmation," *Theology* 49 (1946), pp. 113–18.

E.C. Ratcliff, "The Relation of Confirmation to Baptism in the Early Roman and Byzantine Liturgies," *Theology* 49 (1946), pp. 258–65, 290–95.

H.G. Blomfield, "Baptism and the Catechumenate," *Theology* 50 (1947), pp. 129–31.

J.G. Davies, "The Disintegration of the Christian Initiation Rite," *Theology* 50 (1947), pp. 407–12.

14 See R.H. Fuller, as above note 13.

15 *Baptism and Confirmation*, Prayer Book Studies 1; Church Pension Fund, 1950.

16 Prayer Book Studies 1 (as in note 15) pp. 24–35.

[17] *Holy Baptism With the Laying on of Hands*, Prayer Book Studies 18; Church Pension Fund, 1970.

[18] Two books of essays on Confirmation appeared in this country during the 1960s: Kendig Brubaker Cully, ed., *Confirmation: History, Doctrine and Practice*, The Seabury Press, 1962. *Confirmation Crisis*, The Seabury Press, 1968.

It is significant that the major doctrinal treatments of Confirmation in both books were contributed by Church of England scholars.

[19] As reported in *The Living Church* (November 28, 1971) p. 6.

[20] The changes made by General Convention to the Draft Service did not affect the theology of the rite. For a commentary on the rite see *Holy Baptism*, Prayer Book Studies 26; Supplement by Daniel B. Stevick, Church Hymnal Corporation, 1973.

[21] It has already been thus interpreted by Bishop Wantland of Eau Claire in *The Evangelical Catholic* April 23, 1981.

[22] For a representative expression of conservative evangelical views see *Services of Baptism and Confirmation*, ed. R.T. Beckwith, C.O. Buchanan, and K.F. Prior; Appleford: Marcham Manor, 1967. Also E.C. Whitaker, *Sacramental Initiation Complete in Baptism*, Grove, 1975.

[23] *Alternative Service Book*, SPCK, 1980. It is popularly referred to as *ASB*.

[24] *Baptism and Confirmation To-day*, SPCK, 1955.

[25] *Christian Initiation: Birth and Growth in the Christian Society*, General Synod of the Church of England, 1972.

[26] *The Book of Common Prayer*, 1979, p. 11.

Chapter 2. A Survey of the History of the Catechumenate (Dujarier)

[1] M. Dujarier, "Le catéchuménat et la maternité de l'Eglise" in *La Maison-Dieu* 71, pp. 78–93.

[2] J. Plumpe, *Mater Ecclesia, Studies in Christian Antiquity 5*, Washington, 1943.

[3] K. Delhaye, Ecclesia Mater chez les Pères des trois premiers siècles. Pour un renouvellement de la pastorale d'aujourd'hui, *Unam Sanctum 46*, Paris, 1964.

[4] M. Dujarier, La parrainage des adults aux trois premiers siècles de l'Eglise, *Parole et Mission 4*, Paris 1962.

[5] A. Laurentin and M. Dujarier, Catéchuménat. Données de l'histoire et perspectives nouvelles, *Vivante Liturgie 83*, Paris, 1969, pp. 52–54.

[6] M. Dujarier, "Le catéchuménat et la maternité de l'Eglise."

[7] Ibid., pp. 25–82.

[8] L. Kilger, "Zur Entwicklung der Katechumenatspraxis vom 5. bis 18. Jahrhundert," in *Zeitschrift für Missionswissenschaft 15* (1925), pp. 166–182.

[9] J. Beckman, "L'initiation et la célébration baptismale dans les missions, du XVI siècle à nos jours" in *La Maison-Dieu 58*, pp. 48–70.

[10] J. Christiaens, "L'organisation d'un catéchuménat au XV le siècle" in *La Maison-Dieu 58*, pp. 71–82.

[11] J. Perraudin, "Le catéchuménal d' aprés le Cardinal Lavigerie" in *Parole et Mission 14*, pp. 386–395.

[12] On the history of the renewal in France, see 'Vers un catéchuménat d'adultes" in *Documentation catéchistique 37* (July 1957) which was revised and expanded in "Problémes du catéchuménat," supplement of *Catéchèse*, Paris, 1961. See also J. Vernette and H. Bourgeois, Serait-ils chrétiens? Paris, Châlet, 1975.

[13] For more on this decree, see *La Maison-Dieu 71*.

¹⁴ Ordo initiationis christiane adultorum, Vatican, 1972. In order to appreciate the full significance and the dimensions of the new ritual it is imperative that one be well acquainted with these preliminary studies.
¹⁵ Among the many studies dealing with the new rite, see R. Beraudy, "Le nouveau rituel de bapême des adults" in *La Maison-Dieu 121*, pp. 122–142 and M. Dujarier, "Le nouveau rituel de l'initiation chrétienne des adults" in *Le Calao 21*.

Chapter 3. Baptism and Confirmation: A Relationship of Process (Bray)

¹ Oliver C. Quick, *The Christian Sacraments*, Nisbet & Co., 1946, p. 182.
² J.S. Whale, *Christian Doctrine*, The MacMillan Co., 1945, p. 166.
³ Marion J. Hatchett, *Commentary on the American Prayer Book*, The Seabury Press, 1981, p. 271.
⁴ P.T. Forsyth, *The Church and the Sacraments*, The Independent Press, 1949, p. 214.
⁵ Forsyth, *op. cit.*, p. 218
⁶ Quick, *op. cit.*, pp. 161 ff.
⁷ Forsyth, *op. cit.* p. 223.
⁸ Ernest A. Southcott, *Receive This Child*, Mowbray & Co., 1955, p. 55.

Chapter 4. Some Theological and Pastoral Implications of Confirmation (Parsons).

¹ Murphy Center for Liturgical Research, *Made, Not Born*, University of Notre Dame Press, 1976, p. 54.
² Edward Schillebeeckx, *Christ the Sacrament of the Encounter with God*, Andrews and McMeel, 1963.
³ Leonel L. Mitchell, *Baptismal Anointing*, SPCK, 1966, pp. 10–11 (de Baptismo, 6-7–8).
⁴ J. D. C. Fisher, *Confirmation Then and Now*, Alcuin Club/SPCK, 1978, p. 32. (de Baptismo, 8).
⁵ Murphy Center, *Made, Not Born*, p. 56, Y. Rabanus Maurus, *de Clericoram Institutione*, I, 6.
⁶ *Ibid.*, p. 57, Y. Cyprian, Letter 74, Sections 5, 6, 7.
⁷ *Ibid.*, pp. 68-69, *Summa Theologiae*, III a; 72, 2, ad lum.
⁸ *Rite of Christian Initiation of Adults*, Publications Office, U.S Catholic Conference, 1974, p. 8, par. 34.
⁹ Aidan Kavanagh: *The Shape of Baptism: The Rite of Christian Initiation* Pueblo Publishing Co., 1978, pp. 25–31.
¹⁰ *Ibid.*, p. 28.
¹¹ Gerald Moede, "Ecumenical Pressure and the Mutual Recognition of Baptism/Members." *Mid-Stream: An Ecumenical Journal*, Vol. XVII, No. 3, 1978, p. 261.
¹² *Ibid.*, p. 265.
¹³ *Ibid.*, p. 262.

Chapter 5. The Liturgics of Confirmation (Stevick).

¹ There are many editions of the Edwardean Prayer Books. That in the Everyman's Library series is probably the most accessible. Texts for baptism and

Confirmation rites, with sources, supporting documents, and introductory notes
are to be found in J. D. C. Fisher, *Christian Initiation: The Reformation Period*,
SPCK, 1970. Except for the title just footnoted, spellings are modernized in all
quotations here.

[2] The long and complex story which is summarized here can be traced in full in
J. D. C. Fisher, *Christian Initiation: Baptism in the Medieval West*, SPCK, 1965.

[3] For an analysis of the Edwardean Prayer Books which emphasizes these
matters, see Marion J. Hatchett, "Thomas Cranmer and the Rites of Christian Initiation," unpublished STM dissertation, General Theological Seminary, 1967.
See also Frank C. Quinn, "Contemporary Liturgical Revision: The Revised Rites
of Confirmation in the Roman Catholic Church and in the American Episcopal
Church," unpublished doctoral dissertation, University of Notre Dame Press,
1978, esp. pp. 277-395.

[4] See the facsimile reprint with introduction by Frank V. Occhiogrosso, *A
Catechisme or First Instruction and Learning of Christian Religion* (1570),
Scholar's Facsimiles and Reprints, Delmar, N.J., 1975. Interesting material on
Nowell and his work can be found in John R. Mulder, The Temple of the Mind:
Education and Literary Taste in Seventeenth-Century England, Pegasus, 1969,
ch. 5, pp. 106–129.

[5] Some historical material on catechesis in the modern period can be found in
Daniel B. Stevick, "Christian Initiation: Post-Reformation to the Present Era," in
Made, Not Born, University of Notre Dame Press, 1976, pp. 99–117.

[6] The best account of these matters remains the lengthy chapter by S. L. Ollard,
"Confirmation in the Anglican Communion," which occupies more than half
(pp. 60–245) of the first volume of the old work, *Confirmation*, SPCK, 1926.

[7] The Restoration Prayer Book was the first one to include the bishop's question
to the confirmands: "Do ye here in the presence of God, and of this congregation,
renew the solemn promise and vow, that was made in your Name at your Baptism; ratifying and confirming the same in your own persons, and acknowledg-
ing your selves bound to believe and to do all those things which your God-
fathers and Godmothers then undertook for you." (Text and spelling from 1661).
   The inclusion of adult Baptism for the first time only after a century and a half
of Prayer Book history indicates the way in which (for historically understandable reasons) infant Baptism has been the norm for Anglican theological,
liturgical and pastoral thought and practice. Adult Baptism has been an exception. A church which has its liturgical roots in the early church should be
prepared to think through Christian initiation as an adult rite — of which the infant form is derivative.

[8] Hence the rubric in all American Prayer Books: "And there shall none be admitted to the Holy Communion, until such time as he be confirmed, or be ready
and desirous to be confirmed" (1928 BCP, p. 299). This rubric had been added in
this form in the 1661 English Book to meet the need created by the interruption
of episcopacy and Confirmation during the Commonwealth period. The
"Confirmation" rubric has been dropped altogether in the present Prayer Book.

[9] These matters were faced in Michael Perry, ed., *Crisis for Confirmation*, SCM,
1967. This valuable English symposium contained some chapters which were
applicable to the Episcopal Church. An American adaptation, *Confirmation
Crisis*, was issued by The Seabury Press, 1968. It retained some chapters, deleted
others, and added new material. See esp. ch.1, "Tell It Like It Is," pp. 9–18.

[10] The Introduction to Prayer Book Studies 18 defends the adequacy of this pro-

vision. For a critique see Daniel B. Stevick, "Confirmation for Today: Reflections on the Rite Proposed For the Episcopal Church," in *Worship* 44/9, 1970, pp. 541–560.

11 The point that admission to Communion is to be based on Baptism rather than on Baptism plus episcopal Confirmation was made at the General Convention at Houston in 1970. It has been restated or taken for granted in subsequent actions. The Prayer Book 1979 assumes this history and says nothing whatever on the subject.

12 The text of this statement appears in all printed editions of Prayer Book Studies 26.

13 For the historical and liturgical background of the design of the rite as it appears from Prayer Book Studies 18 to the 1979 Prayer Book, see L. L. Mitchell, "The 'Shape' of the Baptismal Liturgy," in *Anglican Theological Review*, 47, 1965, pp. 410–419. This "shape" is one of the truly brilliant and enduring liturgical developments of the early church. But it is a development. Some important features of it lack clear New Testament or second century evidence. Yet once it took form, it was, and is, a convincing ritualization of faith.

14 One could say that the catechetical component represents the *function* which Cranmer thought of as "Confirmation," but the sacramental component represents the *liturgy* by which he carried out that function.

15 A related aspect of the tension between these two elements is that when one speaks of adolescent Confirmation of persons who had been baptized as infants, emphasis falls on the catechetical rite. But in speaking about Confirmation as a part of the Christian initiation of an adult, one speaks of the sacramental rite.

The requirement that in order to receive the sacramental rite an adult had also to ratify the promises of Baptism seemed to reflect adversely on the seriousness with which one had made those promises—perhaps only days, or hours, or minutes before the bishop's laying-on-of-hands. The rites of the 1979 Prayer Book sought to avoid such redundancies by making it possible for adults to receive the sacramental laying-on-of-hands at the time of their Baptism (and their initial promises). The second rubric on p. 214 (which was added late in the process of adopting the 1979 Prayer Book and was subject to inadequate discussion and examination) reintroduced many of the anomalies of the past in this matter, except when an adult is baptized under the general liturgical presidency of a bishop.

16 The Hippolytean liturgy, which is our earliest model for the post-baptismal ceremonies, was lost for many centuries and is now reconstructed from complex groups of sources. It is interesting to note here that some of the text tradition provides wordings which speak of the seal of the Spirit as given in the water Baptism; other sources support a text which speaks of these gifts as belonging specifically to the bishop's post-baptismal anointing. The evidence is so balanced that modern editors have supported each side. (The matter is summarized in Lampe, *The Seal of the Spirit*, pp. 138–148). There is no need for present-day drafters and interpreters of liturgy to decide this matter critically and then think the thoughts of Hippolytus after him but the existence of this very old difference in the documentary tradition suggests that the relation- between the water moment and the anointing moment in Christian initiation has been variously understood for a long time.

17 This direction can be traced in the titles and contents of, in succession: the early printings of Prayer Book Studies 26, those following authorization by the 1973 Convention, and the form authorized for trial use during 1975–1976. Such

reintroductions of liturgical "business as usual" seem to have had more to do with getting new rites accepted than with arguments of theological or liturgical substance. At no point was a serious rationale for these changes put forward.

[18] This initiatory whole — Baptism, Confirmation, Eucharist — is set forth in *The Book of Common Prayer*, pages 289 to 310. (See also the rubric on page 312 which commends a bishop's visitation as one of the occasions for Baptisms.) The Prayer Book does, however, provide (pages 412 to 419) a fully adequate liturgy (duplicating the relevant portions of the earlier rite) for those occasions when there are persons to be confirmed or received or who are making reaffirmations, but there is no Baptism.

[19] See Marion J. Hatchett, "The Rite of 'Confirmation' in *The Book of Common Prayer* and in *Authorized Services 1973*," in *Anglican Theological Review* 56 1974, pp. 292–310.

[20] See L. L. Mitchell, "The Theology of Christian Initiation and *The Proposed Book of Common Prayer*, in *Anglican Theological Review* 60 (1968), pp. 399–419.

Chapter 6. Christian Initiation, Rites of Passage, and Confirmation (Mitchell)

[1] Mircea Eliade, *Birth and Rebirth*, Harper, 1958, p. x.
[2] Galatians 2:20.
[3] 2 Corinthians 5:17.
[4] I Peter 2:10.
[5] I Peter 2:9.
[6] Eliade, *op. cit.*, p. xiv.
[7] *The Rites of the Catholic Church*, Pueblo, 1976, p. 3.
[8] *Book of Common Prayer*, The Seabury Press, 1979, p. 858.
[9] Arnold van Gennep, The Rites of Passage, University of Chicago Press, 1960.
[10] Dom Bernard Botte, O.S.B., *La tradition apostolique de saint Hippolyte*, Münster: Aschendorffsche Verlagsbuchhandlung, 1963, Liturgiewissenschaftliche Quellen und Forschungen 39, nn. 15–21.
[11] Ambroise de Milan, Des sacrements, des mysteres, ed. Dom Bernard Botte, Sources chrêtiennes 25 bis, Cerf, 1961.
[12] *St. Cyril of Jerusalem's Lectures on the Christian Sacraments*, ed. Frank L. Cross, SPCK, 1960.
[13] *The Rites*, pp. 13–181.
[14] *op. cit.*, pp. 114–116.
[15] *The Book of Occasional Services*, Church Hymnal Corporation, 1979, pp. 112–125.
[16] *The Book of Common Prayer*, pp. 298–313.
[17] *The Book of Common Prayer*, p. 298
[18] L. L. Mitchell, "Christian Initiation: The Reformation Period," In *Made, Not Born*, ed. The Murphy Center for Liturgical Research, University of Notre Dame Press, 1976, pp. 83-98.
[19] *The Book of Common Prayer*, p. 412.
[20] Cf. Urban T. Holmes, *Confirmation: The Celebration of Maturity in Christ*, The Seabury Press, 1975.
[21] *The Book of Common Prayer*, p. 860.
[22] *The Book of Common Prayer*, p. 418.
[23] Cf. Leonel L. Mitchell, "What is Confirmation?" in *Anglican Theological Review* 55 (1973), pp. 201–212; "The Theology of Christian Initiation and *The*

Proposed Book of Common Prayer," in *Anglican Theological Review* 60 (1978), pp. 411–419.

24 Holmes, *Confirmation*, pp. 16ff.

25 Holmes, *Confirmation*, pp. 27–50; Marion J. Hatchett, "The Rite of 'Confirmation' in the Book of Common Prayer and in *Authorized Services 1973*," in *Anglican Theological Reivew* 56 (1974) pp. 292–310; *Commentary on the American Prayer Book*, The Seabury Press, 1980, pp. 251–269; Leonel L. Mitchell, vide supra, n. 23.

26 *The Book of Common Prayer*, (1928), p. 292.

27 *The Book of Common Prayer*, (1928), p. 299.

28 *Constitution and Canons for——the Episcopal Church* (1979), Title I, Canon 16, sec. 3.

29 Daniel B. Stevick, *Supplement to Prayer Book Studies 26*, New York: Church Hymnal Corp., 1973, p. 68.

30 Holmes, *Confirmation*, pp. 25, 57ff, 65ff, 73 et alibi.

31 *Prayer Book Studies 26, Holy Baptism*, New York: Church Hymnal Corp., 1973, p. 4.

32 *The Book of Common Prayer*, pp. 309f, 418f.

33 Holmes, *Confirmation*, p. 65f.

34 *The Theology of Confirmation in Relation to Baptism*, Dacre, 1946.

35 *The Seal of the Spirit*, Longmans, Green and Co., 1951.

36 *The Book of Common Prayer*, p. 308.

37 *The Book of Common Prayer*, pp, 309, 418.

38 Holmes, *Confirmation*, p. 48.

39 "What Does Confirmation Mean?" in *The Anglican* 4.14, Summer 1973, pp. 5f.

40 *Antidote to the Canons on Confirmation III*, quoted from J. D. C. Fisher, *Christian Initiation: The Reformation Period*, Alcuin Club Collections 51 London: SPCK, 1970, p. 255.

41 *The Book of Common Prayer*, p. 412.

42 Michael Perry, *Crisis for Confirmation*, SCM Press, 1967, p. 65.

43 Cheslyn Jones et al (ed.), *The Study of Liturgy*, Oxford University Press, 1978, p. 137.

Chapter 7. Aspects of Childhood Confirmation (Iris V. Cully).

1 Cf. *Will Our Children Have Faith?*, John H. Westerhoff III, The Seabury Press 1976.

2 *Crisis of Faith: The Religious Psychology of Adolescence*, Pierre Babin, Herder and Herder, 1964 and *Faith and the Adolescent*, Herder and Herder, 1965.

3 *Confirmation: The Celebration of Maturity in Christ*, Urban T. Holmes III, The Seabury Press, 1975.

4 *Ready and Desirous: The Report of the Commission on Preparation for Confirmation of the Diocese of New York*, Morehouse-Barlow Co., Inc. 1962, p. 28.

5 *Knock and Enter*, Chad Walsh, Morehouse-Barlow Co., Inc., 1954.

6 *Confirmation Instruction for Eleven-to-Fourteen-year-Olds*, C. William Sydnor, The Seabury Press, 1964.

7 "Our Class was a Call to Action," Patricia Cadwallader, in *The Episcopalian*, March 1981, p. 10. Helpful pre-Confirmation material on the liturgy for younger

children will be found in *We Give Thanks* by Iris V. Cully, Morehouse-Barlow Co., Inc., 1976.

[8] *Confirmation and Education* (Yearbooks in Christian Education), ed. W. Kent Gilbert, "The Purpose of Confirmation Education," C. Richard Evenson, p. 37f., Fortress Press, 1969.

[9] *Ibid*, p. 138.

[10] *The Works of Saint Cyril of Jerusalem*, b. 2, trans. Leo P. McCauley and Anthony A. Stephenson (The Fathers of the Church), The Catholic University of America Press, 1970, pp. 143ff.

Chapter 9. The Parish Context for Confirmation Intentions (Kendig Cully).

[1] For a discussion of parish life as educative see Part Three, "Practice," in *Confirmation: History, Doctrine, and Practice*, ed. Kendig Brubaker Cully, The Seabury Press, 1962, pp. 129–228.

[2] *The Book of Common Prayer*, pp. 415ff.

[3] See the two questions and answers, "What is Confirmation?" and "What is required of those to be confirmed?" in "An Outline of the Faith, commonly called the Catechism," *The Book of Common Prayer*, p. 860.

[4] Examples of such studies would include *Let My People Go: Empowering Laity for Ministry* (Abingdon Press, 1980) and *Management for Your Church* (Abingdon Press, 1976), Alvin J. Lindgren and Normal Shawchuck; *Dry Bones Breathe*, Robert C. Worley, Center for the Study of Church Organization Behavior, 1978; *New Life for Your Sunday School*, Iris V. Cully, The Seabury Press, 1979; *Understanding Church Growth and Decline: 1950–1978* eds. Dean R. Hoge and David A. Roozen, The Pilgrim Press, 1979; *New Hope for Congregations*, Loren B. Mead, The Seabury Press, 1972; *Survival and Mission for the City Church*, Gaylord B. Noyce, The Westminster Press, 1975; *Church Growth Is Not the Point*, Robert K. Hudnut, Harper & Row, 1975; *Strategies for New Churches*, ed. Ezra Earl Jones, Harper & Row, 1976; *Revitalizing the Twentieth-Century Church*, Norman Shawchuck and Lloyd M. Perry, Moody Press, 1982, *The Greening of the Church*, Findley B. Edge, Word Books, 1971.

[5] Consider, for example, the thoughts expressed in the bishop's prayer at Confirmation, *The Book of Common Prayer*, p. 418.

Contributors

Allen F. Bray III, D.D., sometime Headmaster, Christ Church School, Greenville, S.C.

Iris V. Cully, Ph.D., Alexander Campbell Hopkins Professor of Religious Education, Lexington Theological Seminary.

Kendig Brubaker Cully, Ph.D., Dean, The Episcopal Theological Seminary in Kentucky, and Editor, *The Review of Books and Religion*.

Michel Dujarier, Secretary of the West African Bishop's Commission for Catechesis and Liturgy (Roman Catholic).

Reginald H. Fuller, S.T.D., Professor of New Testament, Virginia Theological Seminary.

Leonel L. Mitchell, Th.D., Professor of Liturgics, Seabury-Western Theological Seminary.

Donald J. Parsons, Th.D., Episcopal Bishop of Quincy (Illinois) and former Dean of Nashotah House.

Daniel B. Stevick, S.T.D., Professor of Liturgics and Homiletics, Episcopal Divinity School.

John H. Westerhoff III, Ed.D., Professor of Education and Religion, Duke University Divinity School.